THE RU

A successor t

Steele
Higgins
Harris
Mrs. Beeton
Steadman
Betsy
Boffin
Turvey
Draughtsman
Sutton
Topsy

THE RUBICON FILE

A successor to 'Honeywood'

A. J. Elder

Illustrations by Ionicus

THE ARCHITECTURAL PRESS · LONDON

First published in 1980 by The Architectural Press Ltd : London

Reprinted 1983

ISBN: 0 85139 107 9

Printed in Great Britain by
Biddles Ltd, Guildford, Surrey

Contents

To the late

H B CRESWELL

whose Honeywood file inspired this story

The Principal Characters

Scene Winterfield, a thriving town in the English Midlands during the years 1969–70

The Client

RUBICON LTD.	A growing industrial company involved in the supply of rubber for industry and construction. Originally founded in Italy by an Englishman some fifty years ago (where the Rubicon flows into the Adriatic) the company is now headquartered in the U.K. and is gradually diversifying its products. Rubicon's immediate industrial neighbour in Winterfield is WACC LTD.
GEORGE TURVY MICE MIStructE	Chief Engineer to Rubicon. Aged fifty.
LESLIE DRAUGHTSMAN	Leader of one of Turvy's departments.
J. J. BOFFIN MC MSC	Managing Director of Rubicon. Aged fifty, he has a technical background and is usually addressed as J.J.
REG. 'BOMBER' HARRIS	Site Engineer, referred to by the building contractor as the 'clerk of works.'
MRS DORA BEETON	Rubicon's Canteen Manageress. Aged thirty-five she is a very lively lady and unscrupulous in the nicest possible way.

HORATIO 'PROP' STEADMAN — Rubicon's Works Manager. Aged fifty-five, he is the longest serving member of management and is respected for it.

SIR ISAAC GILDENSTEIN — Chairman of Rubicon. Aged fifty-five, he is an industrial knight with a keen interest in his companies' buildings, especially the interior design on which his wife, LADY GILDENSTEIN, is only too willing to advise.

SIR SIDNEY ROUGH — Down-to-earth successor to the above.

The Architect

RICHARD JAMES SUTTON BA (Arch) RIBA — Possessor and chief protagonist of *The Rubicon File*. Aged thirty-three, he is known as 'Sooty' to warm acquaintances, and married to SUE SUTTON. Depends heavily on the unobtrusive secretarial services of MISS BETZY PARKER. To her efficiency we owe this book.

HENRY HIGGINS MSAAT — Architectural Technician and Sutton's Chief Assistant, which sounds grander than it is because there are only three including himself.

IAN MCDONALD ARIBA AISA — Senior architect to LEVERPULLERS LTD. and Sutton's boss in his last job. Aged forty-three, he is also a good friend to Sutton.

The Quantity Surveyors

CUTT & SHUFFLE — Established twenty-five years ago, this firm of quantity surveyors now has a head office in London which is gradually becoming its real centre of operations.

JAMES LE MESURIER — A Quantity Surveyor working for Cutt & Shuffle. Aged twenty-nine, he is based in Winterfield and is in line for a partnership.

The Building Contractors

KNOTT & BANISTER — Often abbreviated to K & B, this is an old family firm with an enviable reputation for reliability. The Knott side of the business has now died out and the present Chairman and Managing Director is WILLIAM BANISTER, a rather old-fashioned, helpful professional builder.

ALISTAIR STEELE — Contract Manager with KNOTT & BANISTER.

The Sub-Contractors

BLUEPATH GREY & CO. — Steelwork contractors. A large national firm of good repute, with an area manager called S. O. BRACKET.

URIAH HEAP LTD. — Piling contractors in quite a big way.

TOPPS ROOFERS LTD. — Roofing contractors of doubtful repute.

TARRAG LTD. — Roofing contractors of national size.

CORKSCREW BAR CO. — Reinforcement suppliers and structural flooring contractors.

BAINS MARIE LTD.	Kitchen equipment specialists. Their Sales Director is sixty-year old MR STOVER, who is not only a great character in the catering supply business, but something of an epicure.
BROWNING & SKIM	This firm handles floor screeding as well as plastering and is now almost integrated with KNOTT & BANISTER LTD. The Foreman Plasterer is MR W. BUNTER.
BLACKPOOL ROCK ASPHALT CO.	Waterproofing specialists whose area representative is STAN LIMMER. Known in brief as BRAC, this company is not to be confused with the Building Regulations Advisory Committee.
SHEFLEFORD CERAMICS	Fixers of tiles to floors, walls and laboratory bench tops. The Managing Director of this firm is A. C. NORRIMAN, an expert in ceramics and also capable with the tools. His foreman is MR J. CLAYMAN.
GERRY & JOHNS	A well-known and old established firm based in London which specializes in high-quality interior fittings and finishes.
TOUGHGRAIN FLOORS LTD.	Specialists in the laying of cork, vinyl and woodblack floors. Their technical representative is MR E. P. RESIN.
LUXISHEEN LTD.	Paint manufacturers whose representative is MR P. U. RETHANE.
BCP LTD.	A large international chemical manufacturer, supplying industrial adhesives amongst many other allied products. Its technical representative is HERR FRITZ NICHTSCHWINDEN.

Officialdom

I. HARDNUT	A building inspector for Winterfield Borough Council. These days he would be called a 'Building Control Officer'.
DAVID BLORE OBE MC MA (CANTAB)	Secretary of the RIBA.

Introduction

Recently, while glancing through some old correspondence files with a view to discarding them, I found I was reading them as though they were a novel. My curiosity could have been ascribed to the fact I was one of the parties involved, but it struck me there was an inherent interest in the material itself, sufficient to hold my attention even if I had not been concerned in the events at all. Thus the idea followed that these files could be of interest to others.

Inevitably I was reminded of *The Honeywood File*, H. B. Cresswell's comic epistolary novel published in 1924, and it's sequel, *The Honeywood Settlement*. These stories adopted the format of a correspondence file for a job in the office of a young architect of that period, and became reference books for architectural students preparing for the Part III Final. They were, however, also read by a much wider public, not all of whom were architects, nor even connected with the building business. Today, the architect's life bears hardly any relation to what it was in the 1920s and '30s, but the basic principles of professionalism, underlying the architect's relationship with his clients and others, remain fundamentally unchanged.

The story which follows also uses the format of a correspondence file to relate events which together make up the history of a job passing through the office of an architect. None of the incidents or characters bear any relation to those in *Honeywood*, nor, as in *Honeywood*, are they based on any actual incident or person, although some characters may be an amalgam of several people, plus some purely imaginary ones.

The work of a young architect in practice (and possibly a well-established one too) in the 1920s and '30s was often based mainly on private domestic work. The likelihood was that he had spent a little time with a local authority, or as an assistant in private practice and then, taking his courage in both hands, launched out on his own. It was a world, where a young architect, of Spinlove's type and background, could reasonably be expected to succeed, but which offered little inducement (and too much risk) to the majority who saw their best future in serving in local authorities or central government.

After the Second World War the situation began to change. There came a greater demand for the architect's skills than ever before, from a much wider class of client and for a much more diverse range of building types. The need for many more 'sophisticated' buildings in the fields of housing, education, health, industry and commerce, had to be met from a profession trained to deal only with a request for good-mannered, soundly constructed buildings, based on centuries of traditional building practice. The result, for a time, was a great deal of frustration and disenchantment for both client and architect. It is against this background the following story is set.

The quantity of paper required to get a building built has increased beyond belief. I suppose the same has happened in other fields. The architect of the 1920s would be totally bewildered if faced with the legislation, legal problems and technical complexity which today's architect has to face, perforce, in almost every job he does. Once upon a time he worked with simple by-laws which only recognised two types of building, viz. domestic structures and warehouses. There was no planning legislation and building techniques were so standardised that very little was needed in the way of detailed drawings. Everyone knew, for example, how to make a double-hung sash window so all the joiner needed was the overall size. Similarly, Bills of Quantities were so straightforward that I, as an articled pupil of only 3 years standing, was quite capable of taking off. Even so, it seems unlikely that even then the whole of the documents relating to one job could be contained in one file. Cresswell, in fact makes this clear; it was not his intention to suggest any such thing.

Today the documentation for a job the size of Honeywell would probably occupy at least half a filing-cabinet drawer. Thus the correspondence which follows is not intended to be the contents of a single file, but rather a selection of letters from several files which together give a picture of how the job progressed, describing such details as the architect himself might recall if describing the history of the job some years later. In addition, an architect's files (indeed probably most business files) contain a great deal of material in addition to letters.

Such items as minutes of meetings, records of other meetings or events, the content of some telephone calls, and so on. Where these are relevant to the story, they are included. The reader may notice that frequently the reply to one letter follows on the day after it was written. As to this I will only say that the events described occurred before we had a First Class Post, when it was still customary for letters to arrive by the first post on the following day.

The reader may wonder why the action is set in the years 1969–70. This is because at that time, in spite of the complexities I have described earlier, the architectural profession still stood, as it always had, four-square behind its Institute, its Code of Practice, and the spirit of professionalism. Today these values are under fire from many directions, and it is not possible to predict the outcome. Times change and some of our values may sink without trace. We must hope it is not the vital ones. (One of the effects of changing times, unfortunately, is changing prices; and the figures mentioned in this book are those which would have applied in 1969/70. By 1980 prices have quadrupled, and the escalation continues . . .).

And now we start with our hero, Richard James Sutton, hearing from a friend and colleague . . .

I

The Client Appears

IAN McDONALD TO RICHARD SUTTON

Dear Sooty, 3.1.69

Yesterday I had a phone call from George Turvy, the chief engineer of Rubicon Ltd. I don't know whether you ever met him, but as you know they are close neighbours of ours and also tend to align with us on staff, welfare and general policy matters. They are not yet large enough to have their own architect's department and have been using local firms. I use the plural advisedly since they have been through about six firms in the course of as many jobs, and have been totally dissatisfied with the lot. It seems that they are unable to communicate, apparently having no common language.

Turvy wanted to know what we did when we needed outside architectural assistance. Bearing in mind that you could likely do with other clients besides us, I mentioned your name and doubtless you'll be hearing from him soon. I'm not sure if he is as stern a taskmaster as his record suggests, but I believe that with your background and experience you should be able to satisfy him. How about calling in next time you are this way for a wee drappie and to let me know how you got on?

Yours aye,

RUBICON LTD. TO RICHARD SUTTON

Dear Sir, 4.1.69

We recently consulted Mr. Ian McDonald of Leverpullers Ltd. regarding the appointment of architects in private practice. Our experience in the past has been, to say the least, disappointing. Mr. McDonald gave us your name as someone with experience in our field. If you are interested in a project we are about to commence, would you please contact Mr. Turvy's secretary, to arrange an appointment at your earliest convenience.

Yours faithfully,

FILE NOTE OF A MEETING HELD AT RUBICON'S MAIN OFFICES ON 10.1.69

Present:	G. Turvy	Chief engineer
	L. Draughtsman	I/c Drawing Office
	R. J. Sutton	Architect

The meeting was quite informal and no minutes were taken. Present were George Turvy, Rubicon's Chief Engineer, Leslie Draughtsman i/c of the drawing office and myself. Mr. Turvy described the general nature of the firm and its products. The plant at Winterfield is not the only one, but it is the oldest and the company's head office staff are located there (except for the very top brass who are in the 'Great Wen' (sic)). Because of this there is an unusual ratio of staff to pay-roll workers. The staff actually outnumber the rest, roughly about 250 to 200. The projected building is to be part lab., part welfare, and the accomodation to be provided includes a number of quite different purposes which may be difficult to reconcile.

The appropriately named Mr. Draughtsman produced an outline scheme which he had prepared as representing their requirements and this was accepted as an adequate brief from which a start could be made. I sensed a measure of hostility from that direction and formed the impression that Mr. Draughtsman's toes were unwittingly being trodden on, since he felt that his own department could handle the project quite adequately, and perhaps better than any architect.

Existing site plans were produced. Rubicon have detailed plans of the whole of their site and a survey will not be needed. It was agreed that I would get in touch after a couple of weeks which should be long enough for preliminary schemes to be produced. The question of cost was not discussed.

Sutton seems to have a nice compact style for the writing of notes on meetings. It is clear, succinct and covers only the essential ground. There is also a slight touch of levity which helps to brighten an otherwise dull record. Of course, only he and his assistant are going to read it, but even they may feel a little cheered if a track back through the files should become necessary. Let us hope he does as well in his letters.

SUTTON TO RUBICON LTD.

Dear Sirs, 11.1.69

Proposed Laboratory and Welfare Services Building

Following my meeting with Mr. Turvy yesterday, I write to confirm that I shall be most pleased to act for you as architect for the above proposal. Our agreement will be based on the RIBA Conditions of Engagement, a copy of which I enclose. I understand, however, that my authority to proceed is limited at the moment to the completion of the Scheme Design stage.

I have the copy of part of your site plan which you gave me, and I gather this can be regarded as accurate where actual dimensions are shown and also that it is reasonably accurate as to scale. The amount of information shown is such that there should be no need to make a survey.

I am now proceeding to prepare preliminary scheme designs to illustrate possible alternative solutions. There is sure to be more than one acceptable solution. I, of course, already have the scheme put forward by your own drawing office, but I am treating this simply as one way of setting down a schedule of accomodation. I will get in touch again immediately I have some suggestions for discussion.

Yours faithfully,

In spite of his comparatively short experience of private practice Sooty is not doing at all badly. The enclosure of a copy of the RIBA Conditions of Engagement is always a good idea when dealing with new clients and can save misunderstandings later. There are those who would say that he should have gone the whole hog and made direct reference to the scale of fees applicable to this particular project, but there must be a natural reluctance to introduce this rather delicate subject at this stage, before any work has been done. Architects are, after all, supposed to be gentlemen.

The bit about using Rubicon's own scheme just as a schedule of accomodation will not go down too well with Draughtsman who is sure to see it and will no doubt be in charge of the detailed management of the job on the client's behalf.

It was not strictly essential to write this letter at all. He could have left matters until he had something to show. Here again, however, he is showing something of an old head on young shoulders. New clients are not always very keen to issue letters of appointment, and in the absence of such it is well to have something in the record. This leaves the clients with the onus to repudiate anything they disagree with. Apparently there was no reply to this letter.

SUTTON TO MCDONALD

Dear Ian, 11.1.69

Many thanks for your recommendation to Rubicon. They followed it up almost immediately, and I had my first meeting with them yesterday. We seemed to talk the same language. The job itself is not vast, but it is the largest to come my way since I began the practice. What they have in mind is a composite building to house laboratories and welfare services on a rather restricted site, so it is something of a challenge.

Although it was not specifically mentioned, I rather fancy that if I can satisfy them on this job, there will be more to come. They seem to be a go-ahead company and likely to expand considerably. If all goes well I'll be visiting their offices fairly frequently, so I'll give you a ring and call in for a natter sometime soon. Perhaps we could have lunch?

Once again, many thanks for your kindness. Sue also sends her best.

Yours,

As there has been no further correspondence with Rubicon the nxet thing we see is:

FILE NOTE OF A MEETING HELD AT RUBICON'S MAIN OFFICES ON 27.1.69

Present:	G. Turvy	Chief engineer
	L. Draughtsman	I/c drawing office
	S. Bondsman	Welfare and safety officer
	R. J. Sutton	Architect

1. It was agreed that for the sake of brevity the building would be known as the LABWELS building.
2. RJS produced two alternative schemes and described his views as to the relative advantages and disadvantages of each.
3. Both were based on a two-storey structure which would occupy virtually all of the site. There seemed to be no reason why this arrangement should not be used except it would have

"Something like this is what we want . . ."

glazing overlooking a neighbouring works which would not immediately acquire a right of light. GT stated that they were on good terms with their neighbours who would be unlikely to object. However he would put it to them.

4. For the record RJS said that he had received a message to the effect that the small storage building at one end of the site was no longer needed for stores, and it was preferred that this should be incorporated into the new building rather than demolished. This had been done.

5. Basically the schemes were a reversal of each other in respect of the accommodation provided on each floor. Only the client could really decide which would be the most convenient all round.

6. No elevations or sketches were tabled, but RJS pointed out that the great diversity of accommodation types would make the resolution of the elevation problem rather a tricky procedure, if looked at in traditional terms.

7. The client members asked for time to consider the merits of the schemes and to discuss them with others. They should be ready to talk again in a few days.

8. There was some general discussion on programme, detailed design, tender and contractual procedures.

9. The meeting broke up with the next step to be initiated by Rubicon.

The meeting appears to have gone well enough and it seems that Rubicon are not the type to hang about. The introduction of an existing building is interesting as it may have an effect on fees. No doubt we shall find out later.

SUTTON TO TURVY

Dear Mr. Turvy, 28.1.69

LABWELS Building

At informal meetings where no minutes are taken, I usually make notes and circulate these to those concerned (in this case only to yourself). They are accordingly enclosed. If there is anything with which you disagree or think I have omitted please do let me know.

Thank you for a pleasant lunch.

Yours sincerely,

TURVY TO SUTTON

Dear Mr. Sutton, 31.1.69
LABWELS Building

Thank you for yours of the 28th and the enclosed report. I can find nothing in it which requires comment from me, except that you have not mentioned the question of a scheme being prepared in our own drawing office for comparison purposes. This is now ready, and as agreed this morning over the telephone, I look forward to meeting you here again tomorrow to discuss this and, hopefully, make further progress.

Yours sincerely,

Doubtless Sutton had hoped to skate over this one, but he could not really have expected to get away with it. The clash with the ambitious Mr. Draughtsman seems to have come earlier rather than later. This is perhaps as well although it does put a big strain on newly formed relationships, as we shall see.

SUTTON TO TURVY

Dear Mr. Turvy, 2.2.69
LABWELS Building

I am sorry to have left our meeting yesterday to keep another appointment. I want to tell you frankly that this, as you may have suspected, was an excuse. The real reason was that, had I stayed, I might not have been able to prevent myself from saying something I would later regret. Far better for me to write to you in the comparative calm of my office.

At the meeting I was horrified to find that the scheme 'knocked up by one of your draftsmen' was being pressed as a serious contender and that in the event of it being used I would be required simply to process it through to the erection stage. This situation is one I could never accept, nor could any architect worthy of his salt. This would be so even if the design were a good one, but this is far from the case. The scheme simply does not work. The long structural spans are expensive and unnecessary, the circulation is disastrous, and the space allocated to the various functions is in some cases quite inadequate as well as being entirely the wrong shape. The claim that the scheme would be cheaper than mine can only be based on the fact that it is smaller, and is in fact not large enough to meet your requirements. As usual with amateur architects, he also gives us elevations which show a brick facade sprinkled with domestic-type windows, totally unsuitable and out of scale with this type of building, rather like a child's drawing of a house.

I am sorry to have to write in this way, but I hope you will believe me when I say it is entirely in defence of your interests. Architects do not swear a 'Hippocratic oath' but we do operate on the same principles. I hope we can now put this matter aside and concentrate on the development of a properly based detailed design.

I await your comments with some anxiety.

Yours sincerely,

And so he might. Sooty has obviously been driven into a corner from which he could see no escape, to sound off so strongly and so soon after getting a new and highly desirable client. What he says of course, is quite true. Inside every layman is a budding Christopher Wren simply waiting for a chance to show how much better he can do it than the architect. How often one hears the comment 'Oh yes, I designed it myself, the architect merely put my ideas on paper, for planning permission and so on'.

Well, he certainly took a risk, but the fates have been kind and he has got it his way, for next we read:

TURVY TO SUTTON

Dear Mr. Sutton, 9.2.69

LABWELS Building

I was rather startled by the contents of your last letter, and I must admit to some annoyance. In my view you need not have been quite so scathing about the architectural abilities of my technical staff and I find the degree of candour rather inappropriate at this stage in our professional relationship. In fairness, however, I think it is true to say you were placed in a difficult situation, and I accept your assurance that you have our best interests at heart. Perhaps in the past we have tended to try and exercise too much control over our architects. This may have something to do with the traditional lack of understanding between your profession and mine.

On consideration, I have reached the conclusion that we

would be foolish not to accept your outline proposals. I have had a quiet word with Mr. Draughtsman, without showing him your letter, and he now accepts there may be some inherent problems in his scheme.

I have given further consideration to your schemes and discussed the proposals with the works manager and the managing director. As a result, we wish you to proceed on the lines of your Scheme B and come back to us when you have developed the scheme in more detail, including your suggestions for the elevations and an approximate estimate of cost.

Your sincerely,

Turvy has kept Sutton in suspense for a week but Sooty has been lucky in dealing with a man who understands his hurt professional pride. A less patient man might have sacked him. However, he had to take the chance; to continue on that course might have been disastrous. Perhaps this has something to do with Rubicon's record of going through six architects in the course of as many jobs. It rather looks now as though Turvy is going to hold Draughtsman on a fairly short leash to avoid any risk of a head-on crash with Sutton.

There is now an interval during which Sutton is developing his design to what used to be known as Scheme Stage (and still is by many) which means sufficient drawings to fully explain the proposals, including a preliminary estimate of cost. There are a number of notes made following meetings with client and QS, but these are of no particular interest to us. There now follows some correspondence and notes on one particular aspect of the scheme:

2

The Affair of The Curtain Walling

SUTTON TO TURVY

Dear Mr. Turvy, 27.2.69
LABWELS Building

I have now reached the stage where I am ready to submit my scheme drawings etc. for your approval and further instructions. I would much prefer to do this in person so that I can explain the intentions and circumstances which have led to the arrangements as they now stand. I would be grateful therefore if you can give me a date when I can attend and explain the scheme to you and those of your colleagues who might wish to be present.

There is, however, one aspect of the proposals to which I think I should draw your attention now. From the appearance of the more recent buildings on your site I have formed the impression that you (corporately) have a conservative attitude towards building design. You will recall that during discussions I have several times mentioned that the wide diversity of uses to which this building is to be put would make it difficult to create a coherent external appearance. You have expressed a preference for a steel-framed building largely on the grounds that it facilitates the making of alterations in the future should this ever become necessary. You have also requested that the frame be designed to take a future third storey if needed. Thus the external walls will have no structural role, simply one of enclosure. This gives us freedom to adopt one of a number of possible solutions. There are now a number of proprietory systems developed in the main by window manufacturers some of which have been installed for a few years now, so they are not entirely untried. I am suggesting using a module of 40″ (1m) which means that we can subdivide our inside space using any dimension which is a multiple of 40″. This gives us the necessary degree of flexibility, whilst retaining a disciplined external appearance. I can tell you more about this when we meet.

Yours sincerely,

Sutton is apparently anticipating trouble in convincing his client that using curtain walling is a good idea. He is probably quite right, but it was a bit tactless to accuse them of corporate conservatism. It might have been better not to make any special mention of this and hope it would pass unnoticed. Then again, I suspect that by now Sutton is getting his client sized up and knows that this would not work.

If Sutton made any notes following the meeting at which he presented his scheme they were not filed since the next thing we see is:

TURVY TO SUTTON

Dear Mr. Sutton, 3.3.69
LABWELS Building

This is to confirm that at yesterday's meeting your scheme

proposals and preliminary estimate of cost were approved apart from some minor modifications suggested by Mr. Bondsman our Welfare Officer. I will leave it to you to settle these details directly with him. On the question of curtain walling, I think we understand your reasoning, but this is something on which I felt our MD would wish to be consulted and he will almost certainly wish to see some examples in situ. Do you think, therefore, you could arrange for an inspection tour covering say, four or five examples of this form of what I'm afraid I still look upon as walls?

The best time for us would be a week from today and if you will draw up a short list of buildings for us to see, I will arrange for transport. From what you have said the only place we are likely to find several buildings reasonably near together is London. I imagine one day will be enough, but I will arrange for a stop-over of one night after making the tour, returning the following morning.

Please let me know as soon as you have settled details. I suppose that the lack of a firm decision on the curtain walling will have some effect on your programme for production of working drawings etc. but I expect there will be many aspects of the job on which you can make progress. I hope so.

Yours sincerely,

Sutton is probably anxious to press on. He is unlikely to be very stretched and will no doubt be hoping to reach a stage where he can claim some fees. He has in fact already reached such a stage, but he will not want to give the impression that he is living from hand to mouth.

The entry on to the stage of the Managing Director may give our hero some cause for concern. He may not have had a lot of experience of these autocrats, but he has probably had enough to know they are notoriously hidebound in their attitude to architecture (Sutton used the word 'conservative') and tend to make rigid decisions which they oblige their unhappy executives to enforce.

SUTTON TO MCDONALD

Dear Ian, 14.3.69

LABWELS Building

I promised to let you know how I got on with Rubicon in London when we made the curtain wall visit. It got off to quite a bad start because the driver of the hired Daimler didn't know his London well enough. In the rather tense atmosphere that developed, I was able to see that the hierarchical structure of Rubicon is such that everyone is always looking over his shoulder. By great good fortune the situation was saved and the trip went smoothly from there on. Whether or not the Rubicon people (about half of whom have an engineering background) really saw the point of the whole thing is open to doubt, but it was a success for me because on the way home I got my approval to use it. I have an idea it was decided by a show of hands and the majority was small, but enough is enough. I am now cleared for action and up to my knees in paper.

Yours

If Sutton thinks he has seen the last of the curtain wall affair he is mistaken. In the meantime however, he is gaily proceeding with what is the most intensive part of the architect's work, the preparation, not only of the working drawings, but also of enquiries for the various sub-contractors items which will form part of total contract, suppliers items and other routine matters. The most important single matter to be dealt with at this stage is the appointment of a Quantity Surveyor who can offer guidance on the cost of the elements as the architect makes his design decisions. (Some would say this should have been done earlier so that the QS's expert knowledge of costs was available in the early scheme stages. Not all clients, however, are prepared to agree to the appointment of consultants when they don't even know whether they are going to like what the architect will produce.)

SUTTON TO TURVY

Dear Mr. Turvy, 18.4.69

LABWELS Building

Now that we are into the detail design stage. I would like your authority to appoint a Quantity Surveyor who will in due course prepare a Bill of Quantities for tender, and subsequent cost control purposes. Before then, however, his advice will be useful in enabling the cost control procedure to be applied during the development of the design. To leave this until after tenders are received is to court difficulties, as I believe you have found, on occasion in the past.

I would like to put forward the name of Messrs. Cutt &

Shuffle, a well experienced local firm with whom I have worked in the past with satisfactory results. Could I have your approval or comment as soon as possible please?

Yours sincerely,

This was probably dealt with by telephone as there seems to be no formal reply. No doubt Sutton will pick it up when he next writes to his client.

SUTTON TO CUTT & SHUFFLE

Dear Sirs, 20.4.69

LABWELLS Building, For RUBICON Ltd.

This is the code name given to a building to house laboratory and welfare facilities for Rubicon Ltd. at Winterfield. At present I am engaged on the detailed design stage and have the authority of my client to invite you to act as Quantity Surveyors for the project.

If you accept, in addition to preparing the normal bill of quantities for tender purposes etc., I would like your assistance in cost planning the job during the present stage with a view to getting a tender as close to the estimate as possible. My own approximate estimate prepared at early scheme stage is just a little below £100,000.*

I should be pleased to hear from you without delay, when we can no doubt meet to discuss the scheme and its time scale.

Yours faithfully.

Cut & Shuffle, of course accepted with alacrity; quantity surveyors always do. The progress of the job seems to have been reasonable when Rubicon suddenly throw a large spanner into the works. This is in the form of a letter from the Works Manager.

H. STEADMAN TO R. J. SUTTON

Dear Mr. Sutton, 23.4.69

LABWELS Building

You may think it strange that on this occasion I should write to you direct, but it is because I have a distasteful duty to perform, with which George Turvy did not wish to be associ-

* *This would be £250,000 or more today.*

ated. This is simply that the management as a whole, have changed their minds about the use of a curtain walling system on this building. I realise that you (with justification) will think of us as a lot of old fuddy-duddys who should be dragged screaming into the second half of the 20th century, but all I can say to that is, that in the past, we have found that it has paid to eschew methods which have not with stood the test of time.

Of course, I must apologise for having waited six weeks before reversing the original decision, but I am nevertheless sure that the first decision was wrong and even at this stage should be corrected. As you may have guessed, I was not one of those who agreed to the idea in the first place, and since then have felt so unhappy about it that I have tried to get it reversed. My views in the end have prevailed.

I know that as our architect you are going to be very unhappy about it (not the least because you will have to do some of the work over again). In the final analysis, however, the loss of at the most, six weeks, will be a small price to pay to have what we want. Although you may not think so, I believe you may be spared some grief because, had we gone ahead on *your* recommendation, any subsequent faults would inevitably have been blamed on the curtain wall, justifiably or not.

I will leave it to you to settle details of the modifications with George Turvy.

Yours sincerely,

SUTTON TO STEADMAN

Dear Mr. Steadman, 25.4.69

I must admit to a sense of injustice when I received your letter. It was not engendered by the loss of the work already done and the time that goes with it, but more because I really did feel that the solution I put forward was in your best interests. I'm afraid that architects are not noted for accepting the principle of 'the customer is always right'. Rather the reverse; we think that we know better than you, what is in your best interests. There is some justification for this since doctors do not ask their patients on the slab whether they would like plain or purl stitching. The late Frank Lloyd Wright, during an interview, when asked about the client was said to reply 'Ah, yes, the client, poor soul, pour soul'.

". . .it pays to eschew methods which have not withstood the test of time."

Needless to say, I don't subscribe to that philosophy and having adjusted to the new situation will do my best to find a new solution which will be satisfactory to all. I have no doubt that this can be done and although there will inevitably be some delay I will try to keep this to the minimum.

Yours sincerely, c/c G. Turvy Esq.

This must have been a tough one for Sutton to take, but what is he to do? Resign his commission? This would be foolhardy in the extreme because there is no question of fundamental differences being involved. Rubicon has clearly closed ranks, and he has no alternative but to accept with the best grace he can muster. From the date of his reply, it looks as though he spent a day squirming in anguish before accepting his fate and beginning on a new course. In the end Sooty has acceded to the Rubicon decision with some grace, although it is questionable whether he should have risked a degree of levity in his reply to Steadman, whom he has only met two or three times. He must have sized him up as having a sense of humour.

There is a degree of recompense in the penultimate paragraph of Steadman's letter (perhaps a considerable degree) for which he may be very grateful—but of course he will never know.

3
Estimates And Costs

CUTT & SHUFFLE TO SUTTON

Dear Mr. Sutton, 7.5.69

L*ABWELS Building*

I have completed my first assessment of the likely cost of this building based on your revised drawings and specification. The figure I have arrived at is £125,000, which I anticipate may cause you a degree of concern. Of course, I am not working at this stage, from complete information, but I would not expect to be more than 5% out. Translated into a price per square foot (or metre) it does, I admit, sound very high, but we must remember that a high standard of finishes is desirable, if not essential, and there are a lot of costly fittings and services associated with canteens and laboratories, especially the latter.

I have no doubt you will want to do some pruning, and there is some scope for this, but I don't think there is any way of getting down to your original figure, without serious damage to general quality, which is so important in this kind of building.

So that you can consider the options, I am preparing a list of alternatives each of which would show some saving, and I suggest you ring me to arrange a time and date when I can come over and discuss them.

It is good to be working with you again.

Yours sincerely,

This will come as another shock to Sutton. Architects and Quantity Surveyors have quite different approaches to the question of estimates. The architect, not unnaturally, is anxious not to give too high a figure in case he frightens off his client. Thus, if anything, he probably tends to underestimate. The QS, on the other hand, has no such qualms. He seldom comes into direct contact with the client, but supplies the ammunition for the architect to fire. From long experience he knows to allow something for items which the architect may have forgotten (and there usually are some). He also tends to include a larger sum for other contingencies and he likes to leave himself room to manoeuvre, so that at the end of the day, when the final account is settled, he can say, 'There you are, I've saved a little something to give back'.

Not all clients expect 'spot on' estimates, especially in the early stages, but most would regard a 25% increase as representing a degree of incompetence on the part of their architect. Sooty clearly must be very anxious to avoid giving that impression, so he is going to fight hard with le Mesurier to get some reduction.

SUTTON TO CUTT & SHUFFLE

Dear Mr. le Mesurier, 10.5.69

LABWELS Building

I write to confirm the decisions taken during our meeting yesterday. With a view to reducing the cost we agreed a number of amendments, which you are to list and send to me. I hope this can be done very quickly. We also agreed that we should leave out the Contingency sum completely. In reporting to my client, I shall of course make it clear that the estimate is sans contingency, but I think, on balance, this will be a better course enabling me to report a figure within a reasonable distance of my original estimate.

I am now going out for quotations from the various sub-contractors, who will represent a considerable proportion of the total cost (at least 50%). I am awaiting clearance from the client of a list of firms I am suggesting, and they are to put forward some names themselves. With any luck I should have the most important prices in about four weeks time, and with this information we should be able to get much closer to the actual cost of the building.

There are certain details on which I still do not have complete information (e.g. laboratory benches and services) but I can get close enough to what I expect to be required for present purposes, and I am anxious to get things moving to avoid delays later.

Yours sincerely,

Sutton has got himself into a mess. Clearly he did not give enough thought to the cost of expensive fittings and fixtures before rushing into print with his first estimate. He is now wriggling to try and avoid the consequences of his own folly. The wisdom of presenting a contingency-free estimate to the client is to be doubted, but Sooty has his back to the wall.

SUTTON TO TURVY

Dear Mr. Turvy, 10.5.69

LABWELS Building

In collaboration with Mr. le Mesurier of Cutt & Shuffle the Quantity Surveyors, and in the light of the more detailed information we now have, I have produced a revised estimate of cost. The new figure is £110,000, and the degree of accuracy anticipated by the QS is + or − 5%. I regret that this is 10% higher than my original figure, but that was based on preliminary information only, and a number of changes have been made since then, not the least being the scrapping of the original curtain walling proposal for the main elevations.

I should also point out that this is intended to represent the actual cost of the building. I hope that nothing has been left out, but at the same time there is no padding of any kind, not even a contingency sum.

The work in my office is progressing nicely and I am ready to invite quotations for a number of items of sub-contractors or suppliers work. I would be grateful if you will now return to me the list of suggested names to receive the enquiries, with any additions or deletions you would like to suggest.

With regard to the programme, I have found in the past that in order to maintain progress on the site, once the contract has started, it may be necessary to place orders for some of the work before a main contractor has been appointed, especially where an element of design is involved (e.g. the steel frame). This can be done by means of letters of intent, subsequently transferring the order to the Main Contractor. Perhaps I could speak to you about this sometime soon?

I am proceeding on the assumption that the revised estimate is acceptable to you.

Yours sincerely,

He is, is he? It may be a little unwise to shrug the matter off so lightly.

In his first paragraph Sutton is being a bit naughty, not to say crafty. Although he does not specifically say so, the implication is that his proposed curtain walling system, which the client turned down would have been cheaper than more traditional construction, whereas the reverse would almost certainly have been the case. This is not worthy of him.

TURVY TO SUTTON

Dear Mr. Sutton, 11.5.79

LABWELS Building

I must admit to some concern after reading your letter of yesterday. While realising that your first estimate was based on a minimum of information we would normally expect a shot a bit closer than 10%. I also note the lack of contingencies, which might mean that we finish up nearer £120,000 than £110,000. This is more than I can sanction off my own bat, and I shall have to speak to the MD about it. He is a little sensitive about the cost of non-productive buildings. As soon as I can I will come back to you with his comments. I am, however, sufficiently confident that he will accept the situation, and I would suggest that you carry on with the project as normal.

I return herewith your list of suggested sub-contractors and you will see that I have deleted a couple of names with whom we have had bad experiences in the past. Some of the others I know, but some are new to me. No doubt you have previous experience of these. I have added a couple of names, and in one case (the steelwork) I suggest you go straight to Bluepath Grey who have done a lot of work for us, both here and elsewhere. They know our little ways which can sometimes drive contractors to despair, if they are not familiar with them.

Yours sincerely,

This could apply to architects too apparently, which would be much worse, because they can't simply tender for another job if they don't like the one they are on.

The upper echelons of industrial management are usually sensitive about expenditure on which there is no visible return. However all was well because next we read:

TURVY TO SUTTON

Dear Mr. Sutton, 13.5.79

LABWELS Building

I was able to speak to the MD this morning and I am delighted to report he immediately sanctioned the additional expenditure. In addition to the contract sum, we shall of course need to find money to pay for your services and those of the Quantity Surveyor. Although it has never been mentioned, I assume that you will not require the services of any other consultants. We prefer not to become involved with these. I know that both you and the Surveyors have mandatory fee scales to which you must adhere, but I would be obliged if you can give me some idea as to how much they will amount to assuming the work goes through to completion.

Now the job is well underway, I propose to hand over direct responsiblity to Leslie Draughtsman whom you have met on several occasions. It will be his job to co-ordinate things on our side, and all queries and communications should be channeled through him. Of course, I shall still be available for consultation whenever necessary.

Reverting to fees, it must be time you claimed a first install-

"To fees, it must be time you claimed a first instalment."

ment, and if you will let me have this I will see it is dealt with promptly.

Yours sincerely,

It seems that Sutton has another good friend in Turvy. It is not often that people offer to pay before being asked .Of course, it is not his own money which makes quite a difference. Sutton has also got confirmation of the acceptance for his revised estimate so it has been quite good a day for him. I envisage a little celebration party for the Suttons that night.

SUTTON TO TURVY

Dear Mr. Turvey, 15.5.69

LABWELS Building

Thank you for your letter of the 13th. I was naturally relieved to learn the revised estimate had been accepted without comment. To deal with the question of fees, these are clearly set out in the RIBA Conditions of Engagement, another copy of which I enclose for your information. In it I have marked those items and scales which apply in this case. As you are aware, there is a comparatively small amount of alteration work in this project, where the new extension links up with the existing building, and the alterations within the existing building itself. The scale for alteration work is higher than that for new buildings and it will therefore be necessary to put a value on this. The QSs should be able to help us there. In the meantime, I have ignored the alteration element and based this interim account on new building work valued at £110,000.

The account itself is enclosed and it shows the anticipated total for architect's fees. The amount of this claim is based on having reached Part D of the normal service, when 35% of the total fee becomes due. I propose to leave the question of out-of-pocket expenses until the end of the job.

The QSs will not wish to submit an account at this stage. Their usual practice is to wait until tenders are received when they have a definite figure to work on. I have, however, asked them to write to you direct enclosing their fee booklet and giving an estimate of what their total fee will be in respect of both pre- and post-contract services. As this is their first claim, perhaps you would care to tell me how you would like this to be handled. They could submit claims to you direct, but perhaps you would prefer them to be channeled through me?

Yours sincerely,

An architect always feels he is treading on delicate ground when submitting his first account for fees, especially with a new client. Perhaps this is why Sooty has left it so long, since he is already well past stage D (detailed scheme design). He has done quite well, but Turvy might feel a little anxious about the mention of extra fees for alteration work and out-of-pocket expenses.

Most architects would prefer that quantity surveyors' fees be paid direct by the client. The RIBA's Conditions of Engagement state, 'Independent consultants and quantity surveyors should be nominated or approved by the architect in agreement with the client. They should be appointed and paid by the client.' In this case the appointment was actually made by the architect, but with the client's approval, so perhaps this is just splitting hairs. Some clients do wish everything to be channeled through the architect, so they only have one person to deal with. On the other hand, some see the quantity surveyor as their own safeguard against the 'notoriously spendthrift architectural profession'. The QS however, knows on which side his bread is buttered. At least 90% of his work probably comes via architects. I recollect an architect once who had an agreement with the QS he normally used, that he should receive one third of all fees earned on work he introduced, in return for the opposite situation (i.e. he would pay the QS one third of all fees he earned on jobs introduced by him). Needless to say, the architect scored heavily and probably broke the Code of Practice into the bargain.

4
Leslie Draughtsman Takes Over

SUTTON TO DRAUGHTSMAN

Dear Mr. Draughtsman, 15.5.69

LABWELS Building

Mr. Turvy has informed me that now things are well underway with the detailed design of this building, he has asked you to take over the co-ordination of information and instructions within your own organisation, and that I am to approach you (and vice versa) whenever decisions are required from whatever source within the Rubicon organisation.

So far I have worked on approximate information supplied by yourself, Mr. Turvy or others at briefing meetings. This has been adequate during the previous stages of the job, but I am now involved in the internal design details, for which I need detailed briefing from those who are to be responsible for the services to be provided within this building. As I see it this will involve research, general welfare and canteen services.

I would be grateful if you could arrange for each department to produce a list of their detailed requirements, and as soon as possible arrange for a meeting, or meetings, to discuss these. I am not quite sure whether it would be best to have one meeting at which all departments are represented, or, initially at least, to have separate meetings, which would at least have the virtue of not wasting other people's time.

I look forward to hearing from you shortly.

Yours sincerely,

No doubt Sutton will approach Draughtsman with caution, bearing in mind the previous clash of ideas as to the architect's function. There is no record of any reply to this letter, so presumably (and conveniently) the requested meeting(s) were arranged by telephone. Next we see this:

DRAUGHTSMAN TO SUTTON

Dar Mr. Sutton, 20.5.69

LABWELS Building

Following our recent meeting with Dr. Science, our research director, I have as agreed obtained details from members of his department, regarding the lab. fittings, fixtures and services required in the new research lab. I now enclose a drawing showing the layout needed to fulfil these requirements, with notes as to the type of construction and finishes required. Also enclosed are several drawings from a previous project which should be of assistance in preparing your own. I am working on a specification for the various services required and will send this shortly.

I have arranged a meeting with Mr. Bondsman, our welfare officer and Mrs. Beeton the canteen manageress, for 10 am on

23.5.69. If this is not convenient please let me know.
Yours faithfully,

Draughtsman's letter is unlikely to please Sutton since he is again encroaching into the architect's design field. We might well wonder whether this is deliberate, but there are draughtsmen (in the general sense) who can only think with a T square in their hands. Sutton's annoyance shows through in his next letter.

SUTTON TO DRAUGHTSMAN

Dear Mr. Draughtsman, 21.5.69
LABWELS Building

Thank you for your letter and the enclosed drawings. These will be most helpful, but it was not really necessary for you to produce a suggested layout for the lab. furniture. It will serve, however, as a statement of the requirements, despite the fact it leaves quite a few blanks. I attach a list of queries for you to answer, or perhaps you could put me in touch with someone who can. The latter would be probably the best course as it avoids double handling of information, with the extra possibility of errors which this inevitably implies.

In the meantime, I am working on a layout for the furniture which will shortly be available for approval or comment by Dr. Science.

Yours sincerely,

This should pin Draughtsman's ears back without making him too angry. He clearly requires firm handling, but Sutton has to realise that he is going to be stuck with him right through to the end of the job and perhaps beyond. He will also have in mind the scent of further work in the future, a great incentive for him to establish, and keep, good relations with the client body.

FILE NOTE OF A MEETING HELD AT RUBICON LTD. ON 23.5.69 TO DISCUSS CANTEEN AND CHANGING ROOM PROVISION

Present:	Mr. Stephen Bondsman	Welfare officer
	Mr. L. Draughtsman	I/c drawing office
	Mrs. Dora Beeton	Canteen manageress
	R. J. Sutton	Architect
	Miss Betzy Parker	Secretary

1. It was confirmed that the hierarchy of dining rooms as laid down in the original brief still stands, but there are some changes in the numbers of these. There is also to be a change in the amount of space per diner, as a result of visits made by the welfare officer to other canteens. Details of these changes are attached. It is not anticipated they will create any structural problems.

2. Mr. Sutton produced a sketch layout of kitchen equipment based on the experience he had acquired whilst with Leverpullers Ltd. In general both Mr. Bondsman and Mrs. Beeton thought it would meet the requirements quite well, but both had reservations on some of the detail. The impression was, that quite apart from the architect's opinions, they were going to have difficulty in agreeing between themselves. They asked for time to study the proposals in more detail before finally approving a definite layout.

3. The nature of the site and its surroundings meant that it would not be easy to provide adequate ventilation, something absolutely vital to the smooth running of the kitchen. Mr. Sutton outlined his proposals for this which provided for an air change rate of 60 per hour (or one a minute). Mr. Bondsman thought this excessive and that it might create more problems than it solved, but it was agreed to shelve the matter until it could be looked at in more detail when the H and V contractor had been appointed.

4. The early appointment of a kitchen equipment supplier was discussed and it was agreed that this should go out to tender. Mr. Bondsman asked that the enquiry should go to Cass and Erole Ltd. and Bains Marie Ltd. Mr. Sutton said that he had had good service from Benjamin Butler Ltd. on jobs done for Leverpullers. It was agreed that all three should be asked.

5. There was some discussion on the quality of equipment to be provided. Clearly the client's staff wanted perfection, but Rubicon would not be prepared to pay for it. They are to make a selection from catalogues they already have which can be used as a guide for the specification which will go out for tenders.

6. Mr. Sutton also produced a suggested layout for the changing and washing facilities. Some changes were suggested and there will be no problems in implementing these. Revised drawings will be sent for approval in due course.

The 'hierarchy of dining rooms' mentioned in note 1 are not defined, but from our privileged position we can get a glimpse of the 1/100 floor plans and find there are in ascending order, a pay-roll dining room, staff dining room, senior staff dining room and Chairman's dining room. It is the last that Sutton will have to keep a wary eye on.

5
Mrs. Beeton Has Her Say

MRS. BEETON TO SUTTON

Dear Mr. Sutton, 25.5.6

I know that all communications with you should be routed through Mr. Draughtsman, but I am taking the unusual step of writing to you direct because I have problems within my own department here that you may be able to help with.

My problem really is Stephen Bondsman our welfare officer. His background has been in fire and safety matters and he knows nothing whatever about the catering business, whereas I learned my trade in the hotel field. However, like some men, (I am quite prepared to exclude some) he thinks that male brains are always better than female ones, and seems to take a delight in over-ruling me on every possible occasion. You may have noticed a tense atmosphere when we had our recent meeting. What I am very worried about is that the kitchen as now planned could turn out to be a disaster and the girls may refuse to work with some of the equipment specified.

You could help me by pointing out to Bondsman certain things, which in *your* opinion are unlikely to work well. After all, as an architect with prior experience of this type of building, your opinion must count for something. I presume that, in any event, you will have your own views about the layout which may coincide with mine, but no one who has not had the experience of actually running a large kitchen, can fully understand the importance of having the right equipment in the right place.

If you are agreeable perhaps you can come to my office, where I think an hour or so's talk would be long enough for me to explain the changes I would like to have.

Yours sincerely,

SUTTON TO MRS. BEETON

Dear Mrs. Beeton, 26.5.69
LABWELS Building

Thank you for your letter. As you must realise this puts me in rather a difficult situation in relation to other senior staff members with whom I have to work, as it cuts across my instructions as to lines of communication.

Having said this, I am in no doubt as to my duty with regard to the layout of your kitchen. Only an idiot or a rogue would deliberately ignore the advice of someone as experienced as you, so that whatever the circumstances I shall make it my job to see, if at all possible, that you get the layout you want. To do so I will, as a first effort, do as you suggest, and put forward revised proposals to Mr. Bondsman. If this fails I shall consider what further steps I should take.

I look forward to meeting you tomorrow, in your office, to discuss the proposals, and at this stage I don't intend to mention our discussion to anyone else.

Yours sincerely,

As we have seen before, Sutton is very conscious of his professional duty. In fact, with a little more experience one suspects he could become a bit of a bore on the subject. Anyway, he is facing up to an awkward situation in really quite an impressive manner.

The letter is, of course, for Mrs. Beeton's eyes only, but one never quite knows where correspondence may get to. The reference to 'an idiot or a rogue' was a little incautious, since it could, in the context of the letter be interpreted as referring to Bondsman.

SUTTON TO DRAUGHTSMAN

Dear Mr. Draughtsman, 30.5.69
LABWELS Building

Since the meeting we held recently to settle details of the kitchen layout and other matters, I have had some further thoughts on the subject of the kitchen equipment, which led to my checking back on a previous job. As a result, I would like to propose some changes, which I am certain would result in more efficient working.

I enclose three copies of a drawing and a list of the equipment required for this new layout. The extra copies are for Mr. Bondsman and Mrs. Beeton and I would be grateful if you would canvas their views as soon as possible, as we really should be out for tenders now, as I know that some of the items are subject to long delivery periods.

Yours sincerely,

RECORD OF TELEPHONE MESSAGE

Time 11.30
Date 2.6.69
From Mr. Bondsman of
Rubicon Ltd.

Mr. Bondsman said that he had received your revised scheme for the kitchen layout, but that he won't approve it. He said that he was quite happy with the original scheme and saw no point in throwing everything into a turmoil by changing it now. You are to proceed on the old basis. He sounded a bit annoyed.

Bondsman has clearly smelled a rat. Sutton is now in trouble and has simply been caught in the no-mans-land between two warring factions. He cannot just ignore Bondsman's instructions, but equally, he cannot act on them since he is satisfied that they are against the best interests of the client. He has to seek help elsewhere, and this he does.

SUTTON TO TURVY (STRICTLY CONFIDENTIAL)

Dear Mr. Turvy, 3.6.69
LABWELS Building

I am sorry to trouble you, but I feel the problem I am about to outline should come direct to you rather than via Mr. Draughtsman.

We had a meeting recently to sort out the kitchen layout and equipment. Both Mr. Bondsman and Mrs. Beeton, being the two persons most closely concerned, were present, and at the conclusion I thought we had reached agreement. A day or so later, I was surprised to receive a letter direct from Mrs. Beeton which placed me in a difficult situation. It appears that she and Bondsman do not hit it off, and she claims that he deliberately tries to frustrate her efforts. In this particular case the layout I thought had been agreed by all parties is apparently hopelessly out of line with her requirements, and she must be the person to know what is best. Having looked at the changes she proposes to make, I have to admit I think she is right, and I have gone so far as to say that I will do my best to see them implemented, as I think this would be in Rubicon's best interests.

What I did, therefore, was to prepare a revised layout and specification, and sent them to Mr. Draughtsman with copies for Mr. Bondsman and Mrs. Beeton, suggesting it was better than the original scheme, but without mentioning Mrs. Beeton's letter. Unfortunately this did not work because Mr. Bondsman passed a message by telephone to my secretary to the effect that he wishes me to proceed with the original scheme.

If I accepted that, for the sake of an easy life, I would not be able to live with my conscience, and so I decided that my best course would be to acquaint you with the facts and ask if you could help. I cannot serve two masters, especially when they both want different things.

Yours sincerely,

TURVY TO SUTTON

Dear Mr. Sutton, 5.6.69

LABWELS Building

I am very sorry to learn you have been placed in such an untenable position because of some internal nonsense on our side. I found an opportunity to have a word with the MD about it, and it appears this particular little squabble is not altogether unknown to us. He had already been considering a change in the order of command and this has convinced him that it is necessary. What is to happen is that the Works Canteens will no longer form part of Welfare (which is having to be enlarged in other directions) and will come under the direct control of the Works Manager, (who will leave it to Mrs. Beeton).

You can therefore safely proceed with your revised scheme as approved by the Manageress. Leslie Draughtsman has been told of this change and will see that it is followed through. For details of the other welfare facilities you will still need to deal

"That time-hallowed repository for bottles, the top drawer of the filing cabinet."

with Mr. Bondsman (through Leslie) but I think you will find that things will progress smoothly.

Yours sincerely,

The implication of the last sentence is that Bondsman has been told to cool it, and has probably been given a sop in the shape of some additional responsibilities elsewhere. He must suspect that he has been framed but all is well and the last word is, as ever, from the lady.

MRS. BEETON TO SUTTON

Dear Mr. Sutton, 6.6.69

I felt that I really had to write and thank you for the splendid way you rallied to my assistance. I am, believe me, most grateful, not only for the way you solved this particular problem, but also because you seem to have managed to remove future difficulties too. I am so glad things have turned out this way.

No doubt we shall be seeing more of each other as the work progresses and I shall look forward to collaborating with you. The next time you are round this way, why not drop in for a nice chat and a drink. You know where my office is. I am nearly always in around 12 noon and we can open that time-hallowed repository for bottles, the top drawer of the filing cabinet!

Yours very sincerely,

6

Bluepath Grey Try It On

SUTTON TO CUTT & SHUFFLE

Dear Mr. le Mesurier, 30.5.69

Rubicon LABWELS Building

You will remember that I have received instructions from the client to go direct to Bluepath Grey for the steel frame. Apparently they have had good relations in the past. Accordingly, I sent them a set of my drawings, and have now received from them their own design drawings and a quotation. It is the latter that perturbs me, since it is about 33% higher than the sum allowed in your estimate (which I also thought was about right). I realise we can't expect to be dead right on every item in the estimate, and there are usually swings and roundabouts, but this particular swing is too large to be balanced by any likely roundabouts. I have considered going out for another price (or prices) for comparison purposes. What do you think?

Yours sincerely,

Sutton does seem to be getting more than his fair share of trouble from this client, but he is probably not surprised. Large firms, like Rubicon which have frequent reason to use the services of the construction industry, tend to build up relationships with firms they feel they can trust, and of course they know them much better than the architect, whose first job this is. If he gets a second job he will probably find the going much easier.

Rubicon probably know they are paying a bit over the odds for their steelwork, but don't mind because they are getting what they want, when they want it. They probably don't realise, however, how much more they are paying. In any case if they are aware of this, they might at least have warned Sutton to add something to his estimate for this special situation. (They themselves probably add a substantial sum before presenting estimates to the board. I know of one large corporation where this amounts to 25% and is referred to as 'Contingencies and works general charges).

LE MESURIER TO SUTTON

Dear Mr. Sutton, 3.6.69

LABWELS Building

I have looked into the matter of the steelwork price and am satisfied there was no error in my figures. Furthermore, steel is one item where we can expect a high degree of accuracy, thus it seems that Bluepath Grey are cheating a bit. They must feel very secure. The question is what can we do about it?

In general, no one likes the practice of seeking quotations from specialist firms (especially where calculations are involved) when there is no intention of placing an order with the lowest tenderer. In this case, however, I think the result justifies the means. The alternative is for us to simply report our findings to the client and ask for instructions. One or more actual prices would be more convincing.

Yours sincerely,

We are beginning to see a spark of humanity in le Mesurier, which is unusual in a quantity surveyor. The use of the plural 'we' and 'us' implies a willingness to share responsibility in a team spirit. In the past I have found the team spirit dwindling rapidly when any form of trouble rears its ugly head.

His advice, however, is bad. The best course would have been to report the situation to the client without delay. The other alternative would be to simply forget it, and there are many that would have done so. Sutton, however, is made of sterner stuff, as we have seen in the past. (Those who view the architects' mandatory fee scale with a jaundiced eye, would also point out that increased price results in increased fees, but it can be truly said that such a consideration never affects the architect's judgement; on the contrary he will fight, and fight again in a never-ceasing battle, to keep his clients costs to the minimum.) Two enquiries did go out with the following results:

RIVET & CLEAT TO SUTTON

Dear Sir, 5.6.69

RUBICON LABWELS

Thank you for your esteemed enquiry of even date. We regret that at the moment we are not in a position to take any further orders because of a full book and scarcity of rolled steel. We would still be pleased to receive any further enquiries from your office for work in the £5000–50,000 bracket.

Yours faithfully,

Admirably brief and to the point, this reply came back like a boomerang: There are those who would have waited two weeks and then submitted a price which could not succeed, under the impression that not to tender will take them off the architect's list for future enquiries. This is generally not true and architects prefer the honest approach. A day later, the other firm replied.

THE BOLTON ERECTION CO. TO SUTTON

Dear Sir, 6.6.69

Rubicon Labwels Building

Thank you for the enquiry regarding the steelwork for the above building. Because of certain unhappy experiences we have had in recent months we have made it a rule only to tender when the enquiry is accompanied by a list of all the other tenderers. If you will supply us with such a list we shall be happy to let you have our quotation.

We are, yours faithfully,

This is an unheard-of request. It is not unusual for an architect to send a list of firms who have tendered to each of them showing the results, but not to send a list with the enquiries. It may well be possible for firms to find out who else is on the list through their own trade organisations and in the past this sometimes led to the pernicious practice of 'borrowing' a price, whereby a contractor who was not interested simply rang one who was, and got a figure from him that was safely above the genuine offer.

Can it be that Rivet & Cleat and Bolton Erection are privy to the arrangement that Bluepath Grey have with Rubicon and are loyally staying out of the battle? It seems suspiciously like it, although the reference to 'unhappy experiences' in Bolton Erection's letter could refer to an occasion when they may have tendered against Bluepath Grey in the past and had been rejected although their price was known to be lower. Nothing upsets a contractor more than this and understandably so. Sutton is now no further forward, but there is another letter to come.

BLUEPATH GREY TO SUTTON

Dear Sir, 8.6.69

Rubicon Ltd., LABWELS Building

Now that you have had our scheme and quotation for some little time, we would welcome the opportunity to discuss these with you. Apart from the question of price, there is the important matter of programme to be discussed. This will depend mainly on how soon we can expect to be on site, and the delivery dates we can expect from our suppliers for the necessary sections. Being part of a much larger organisation, we are in a better position than most in this respect.

As you may know we have, in the past, done a lot of work for your clients Rubicon Ltd., we believe to their satisfaction. As we have not previously had the pleasure of working with you, may we suggest that our area manager should call on you to discuss the job in general. A suitable time and date for him would be 11 a.m. on 12.6.69 and we hope this is convenient to you. Mr. Bracket (our AM) would be pleased if you would join him for luncheon afterwards.

Yours faithfully,

This is flannel. If Bluepath had really wanted to discuss technicalities, they would have sent a technician. Bracket probably doesn't know a bending moment from a section modulus. His main concern will be in keeping up his order book and making a profit. Sutton smells a rat and decides to move with caution.

SUTTON TO BLUEPATH GREY LTD.

Dear Sirs, 9.6.69

LABWELS Building for Rubicon Ltd.

Thank you for your letter. The time and date you suggest are convenient to me and I shall expect Mr. Bracket then. Unfortunately I have another engagement at lunch time.

Yours faithfully,

He doesn't of course, but is shy of placing himself under any obligation whatever until he finds out what makes them tick. Not that there is anything wrong with the ordinary business lunch, and many problems have been solved over the dining table. However, there are occasions when they could be loosely called a bribe. There was no need for Sooty to be quite so curt; after all he is going to have to work with them (or perhaps he doesn't think so?)

SUTTON TO LE MESURIER

Dear James, 9.6.69

LABWELS

I have a meeting with Bracket of Bluepath Grey fixed for 11 a.m. on the 12th. Ostensibly he is coming to discuss technicalities, but I suspect his motives. Would you care to come along and sit in on it?

Yours,

NOTES DICTATED AFTER A MEETING AT THIS OFFICE TO DISCUSS ARRANGEMENTS FOR THE LABWELS STEELWORK CONTRACT ON 12.6.69

Present:	Mr. S. O. Bracket	Area Manager, Bluepath Grey
	Mr. le Mesurier	Quantity surveyor, Cutt & Shuffle
	R. J. Sutton	Architect

1. Mr. Bracket started by saying he had asked for the meeting simply to get to know people he had not previously worked with, and to discuss the job only in very general terms.

2. He stated that since his letter, he had put in hand the ordering procedure for the steel and that prospects for early delivery were quite good. He made the point, however, that early deliveries involved extra cost, because they were unable to shop around for the cheapest stockist. He also said that Rubicon were aware of this and that his usual contact there was Leslie Draughtsman.

3. R.J.S. reminded Mr. Bracket that so far no order had been placed and that any material ordered now would be at Bluepath's own risk. Mr. Bracket said that, after their long and happy relationship with Rubicon, they were prepared to take risks of this type in the interests of good progress. He had no doubt that the order was a formality.

4. There followed some discussion on programme from which it emerged that anticipated site dates could be met (just).

5. Bracket then introduced the question of prices. He had been a little uneasy about the total price for this job and had instigated an enquiry. It appeared that the estimator had included one complete row of columns and beams which did not exist, a mistake so basic it had been very easy to overlook, even when double checking. The effect of this was to reduce the total price by about 16%. He was pleased to have discovered the situation before anyone else, or suspicion might have been aroused (too true).

It is now clear that Bluepath have been sticking it on. They deserve to be properly exposed, but neither Sutton nor le Mesurier want to stir things up, providing they are satisfied that the client is getting reasonable value for his money. With the adiustment that Bluepath are now prepared to concede, the price is only about 12% higher than a proper competitive tender. This is obviously a carefully judged figure and the extra 12% is about what one would expect for the privilege of getting prompt service. In view of this it is not surprising that Sutton and le Mesurier decide to call it a day and quietly recommend acceptance of this quote by the client. To sour relations between a client and a contractor, who previously had good relations, would be of no benefit to anyone and Bluepath Grey will certainly be more careful on any job run by Sutton in the future. They will not have missed the significance of Sutton's rejection of luncheon with Bracket, or the presence of le Mesurier at the meeting. They apparently followed this up with an official revised quotation which was accepted.

SUTTON TO BLUEPATH GREY

Dear Sirs, 16.6.69

Rubicon Ltd. LABWELS Building

Thank you for your revised quotation dated 14.6.69 for the steel frame to the above building. This is acceptable to my clients and you are requested to accept this as a letter of intent to proceed with the contract. You may also regard it as your authority to proceed with the ordering of the material and any work needed prior to arriving on site. The main contract will be in accordance with the RIBA Conditions of Contract*, and when a main contractor has been appointed, he will be instructed to place his order for the steelwork with you in accordance with this letter and your quotation.

If you have any questions regarding this procedure, please do not hesitate to contact me.

Yours faithfully,

This is a useful procedure when a long-delivery item forms part of a contract and can often avoid delays on site when architects have not been as far-seeing as Sutton. This is probably one of the reasons why Sutton's predecessors failed to impress Rubicon.

The last sentence suggests that Sutton has had sub-contractors in the past who have not been too happy with this arrangement. To maintain good progress it is absolutely vital to arrange at least some of the sub-contracted work during the design stages before the identity of the main contractor is known. However, this can put the sub-contractor in a tricky situation because relationships between certain sub and main contractors are not always cordial.

7
Trouble with the 'Regs'

SUTTON TO WINTERFIELD BOROUGH COUNCIL (ENGINEER'S DEPT.)

Dear Sirs, 9.6.69

Laboratory and Welfare Building for Rubicon Ltd.

I have your notice of rejection of the application for per-

*Today this would be the J.C.T. form of contract.

mission to erect this building, which gives the grounds for rejection as 'Non-compliance with Regulation A10, Schedule 3'. As you are aware this is simply the general clause regarding the type and number of documents which must be supplied to enable the local authority to determine whether or not the proposals comply with the Regulations. It gives me no assistance in locating the part of the Regulations on which you require more information. Could you supply a list please?

Yours faithfully,

I. HARDNUT (BUILDING CONTROL OFFICER) TO SUTTON

Dear Sir,

Laboratory and Welfare Building for Rubicon Ltd.

We acknowledge receipt of your letter of 9.6.69 regarding grounds for rejection of your application for permission under the Building Regulations to erect the above building.

You should understand that the onus of proving that any building will comply with the Regulations, is on the applicant. The local authority has a duty to approve or reject applications, but not to do the applicant's work for him by spelling out in detail where the application falls short.

However, in the interests of good relations, we are prepared to discuss this with you at these offices, by prior arrangement.

Yours faithfully,

This is not untypical of the unhelpful attitude of some Local Authorities entrusted with the duty of enforcing the Building Regulations. This used not to be so, except in rare cases, and the new sensitivity is almost certainly the result of one or two cases which reached the courts, in which certain building defects were found to indicate negligence on the part of the building inspector who had a statutory duty to draw attention to such a defect, at the time it was built. In one case where settlement had occurred, the intention of the owner had first been to sue the builder, but he had gone bankrupt, then the architect, but he had inconveniently died. This left the local authority as the next legatee in line. Thus, local authority employees are now much more inclined to 'work to rule' and we have all seen the sort of chaos that results, when this happens in commerce or industry.

SUTTON TO WINTERFIELD BOROUGH ENGINEER

Dear Sir, 19.6.69

Rubicon Ltd. LABWELS Building

Following yesterday's meeting with Mr. Hardnut, I write to confirm the items on which you are not satisfied, and the action to be taken to overcome these.

1. Reg. C9: Damp-proof courses in cavity walls. The position and type of these is to be noted in more detail on the drawings, which will then be re-submitted.

2. Reg. D3: Foundations. My own calculations are enclosed.

3. Reg. D8: Structure above foundations. These calculations are being made by the structural steel erectors, Bluepath Grey and Co. Ltd. I have spoken to them and I expect to have them in my hands in a few days time. I will send copies to you as soon as they arrive.

4. Reg. E7: Calculations for the extent of unprotected area. These will be sent to you, as soon as they have been copied in fair hand.

5. Reg. D15: Structural Brickwork. Schedule 7, Rule 11 (3) Cavity walls. We failed to reach agreement on this. The rule states that the width of cavities must not be less than 2″ (50 mm) nor more than 3″ (75 mm) whereas the cavities in the proposed building are in fact 4½″ (112 mm). My contention is, however, that Schedule 7 was never intended to apply to panel walls between steel framing members. Furthermore D10 Schedule 7 are 'deemed to satisfy provisions' which are not mandatory. To carry out the alterations needed to meet your ruling at this stage would mean virtually redesigning the whole building enclosure and would leave some ugly details. I therefore intend to apply to the Minister for a ruling. Would you please send me the necessary forms.

Since we have now cleared all but one of the problems, I trust you can now place my application before the next meeting of your Development Committee for approval, except for a proviso on the question of the cavity walls. A delay of another month could prove a serious threat to the programme.

Yours faithfully,

The Building Regulations contain the law in the shape of mandatory regulations, and the 'deemed to satisfy' clauses, which give the designer one or more ways of complying, but which do not preclude the possibility of using some other method. To make this quite clear the Regulations themselves are set in normal vertical print and the 'deemed to satisfy' clauses in italics. Both D15 and Schedule 7 are in italics. In spite of this it is not unusual for building inspectors, (now called 'building control officers') to ignore this distinction, especially those whose experience dates back to the days of the Model By-laws, which were not written in the same way. Not infrequently they get their way, and it does make life a great deal easier for them. Why should architects want to mess about with fancy new forms of construction which haven't stood the test of time?

If Hardnut was seriously concerned about the stability of the walls his right course would have been to ask Sutton to demonstrate by calculation or other means that his panel walls are adequately stable. It seems that he is not too bright, but he is going to be a tough nut to crack.

Notice that in his letter Sutton, is asking for a ruling, not a relaxation, because in his view he is not breaking any regulation.

SUTTON TO HARDNUT

Dear Sir, 21.6.69

Rubicon Ltd. LABWELS Building

Further to my recent letter regarding an appeal to the Minister, I enclose duplicate copies of the appropriate form together with the drawings which illustrate the construction to which you object. I would be obliged if you would forward these to the Department, with your own comments as soon as possible.

Yours faithfully,

HARDNUT TO SUTTON

Dear Sir, 25.6.69

B.R. Application ref. no. 776/33/69 Rubicon

Since your last communication I have given further consideration to the question of the cavity walls in this building and have discussed the matter with the Borough Engineer. We have now decided to sanction this construction provided the bricks are laid in compo* and the number of wall ties increased to twice the usual number. It will not therefore be necessary to

**Compo: a name used in the trade for straight cement and sand 1:3.*

forward your appeal to the DoE.

Unfortunately, owing to the delays incurred through the lack of information on your original application, and subsequent decision to appeal, the application lost its place in the queue and it is now no longer possible for it to be included in the agenda for this month's meeting of the development committee, which already has more business than it can process in one night. It will therefore now be held over to the next meeting, just over a month from now.

Yours faithfully,

Hardnut has probably lost his nerve and so as not to lose face is putting the boot in at the place where he knows it will hurt the most. Sutton will be furious and not a little disconcerted. He has pushed on with his enquiries and by now has quite a number of sub-contractors etc. lined up with provisional site starting dates.

He may also be under the misapprehension that he cannot, by law, order a start on site until Building Regulation approval is received. This is not so; his only duty is to ensure that the building when finished does comply with the regulations. Since he has now settled all outstanding problems with the Building Inspector, he would not be taking any great risk in doing so.

Sutton has every reason to feel aggrieved. However, he will be wise not to let it show. He allowed his irritation to show through in his first letter to Winterfield Borough Council on 9.6.69 which read rather as though he was brushing aside some minor irritant and it never pays to patronise. We may well see more of Hardnut.

SUTTON TO HARDNUT

Dear Sir, 26.6.69

Rubicon Ltd. LABWELS Building

Your letter of yesterday's date came as a considerable shock. Having settled all but the one item, I assumed that the application could still go before this month's meeting with your recommendation for approval. Now that you have withdrawn your objection to the 112 mm cavities, there would not have been any need for a proviso.

There are still three days before the meeting and I would ask you to reconsider the possibility of dealing with this application now. This is not some shed or garage extension, but an important building for a growing company who contribute a not inconsiderable share of the rate income of your authority. It is especially important for the staff and pay-roll employees many of whom also contribute to that same income, and who are having to make do with sub-standard accommodation at this time.

I feel sure your elected members would feel the Council has a responsibility to the major employers in its area. Ancillary buildings, which contribute nothing to production capacity are not always regarded as urgent, but perhaps I need hardly say that the well-being of the workforce is an important factor in production, as well as being very important per se (in itself, for its own sake).

Yours faithfully,

Sutton does not give up easily, but he should be careful not to allow himself, as an architect, to get mixed up with local politics.

RECORD OF TELEPHONE MESSAGE

Caller	R. J. Sutton
To	G. Turvy, Rubicon Ltd.
Date	26.6.69 12 Noon
Job	LABWELS

Telephoned G. Turvy re the delay on Building Regs. approval. Explained the situation and the contents of my letter trying to get a slot in this week's meeting. He approved of what I have done and is going to have a try himself. Apparently the MD is on good terms with several of the councillors and regards it as a duty to maintain good relations with the local authority. I gained the impression that the Council may owe him a good turn.

R.J.S.

Whatever is happening behind the scenes, nothing seems to have filtered through to Sutton. Then, after a gap of almost two weeks we read the following:

WINTERFIELD BOROUGH COUNCIL TO SUTTON

Dear Sir, 9.7.69

B.R. Application No. 776/33/69 Rubicon

I have to inform you that at their meeting on the 29th ult.

the Development Committee of this Council approved your application for the above. The form of approval and the stamped copies of your documents are enclosed. Also the site notice cards to be submitted as the work progresses. We shall need at least one week's notice of each inspection stage.

Yours faithfully,

A somewhat graceless letter, but Sooty will not mind that. His persistence has paid off, no doubt with a little gentle lobbying from the MD. Mr. Hardnut is bluffing again. He can't insist on 7 days notice as Reg. A11 specifies only 24 hours, as he very well knows. A touch of pique no doubt.

8

Tender Traps

SUTTON TO FIVE BUILDERS

Dear Sirs, 10.5.69

Laboratory and Welfare Building for Rubicon Ltd.

The design of this building is now well advanced and in approximately one month the Bills of Quantities should be completed. The estimated cost is a little over £100,000 and it is hoped that completion can be achieved in one year from entry on to the site. The site itself is inside Rubicon's plant at Winterfield.

If you are interested in tendering for this project, I would like to hear from you, when I will arrange to send you a set of Quantities.

Yours faithfully,

This is a sensible arrangement. The builders will be grateful to Sutton for giving them a month's warning so they can review their current work load and take into account any other invitations they might expect to receive. All too often, a BoQ lands with a thud on a builder's doormat without any warning, just when he has accepted another invitation to tender for something he doesn't like half as much.

LE MESURIER TO SUTTON

Dear Richard, 10.6.69

RUBICON LABWELS

As I said when we met a few days ago the Bill is complete and has now been printed. It is being despatched today to the five builders on your list, who have been approved by the client. Although I know that Rubicon want to get started as soon as may be, I would not like to allow less than four weeks for pricing. As we both know, undue haste often leads to errors. I enclose a copy of the enclosing letter.

Yours sincerely,

The use of Sutton's Christian name suggests that good inter office relations have been established. Whether le Mesurier knows it or not, the use of 'Sooty' would have been altogether too familiar.

To allow four weeks for pricing a job of this size and complexity is very wise. The contractor's own quantity surveyor has a lot of work to do and parts of the bill usually have to go to the builder's own sub-contractors for pricing. The last sentence suggests that there was some trouble on a previous job with which they were both concerned. We may find, however, that Rubicon are not too happy with the situation. Employers whose business involves engineering skills do not always realise how much more complex the process of putting a building together can be, in comparison with, what is involved in some engineered structures.

LE MESURIER TO FIVE BUILDERS

Dear Sirs, 10.6.69

Rubicon Ltd. LABWELS Building

We are informed by the architect, Mr. R. J. Sutton, that you have agreed to tender for this project. We accordingly enclose two copies of the Bill of Quantities which we have prepared from the architect's drawings. A set of these may be seen at any time within normal office hours at the architect's office or at this address. In your own interest you are advised to visit and inspect the site. Permission for this may be obtained from Mr. L. Draughtsman at Rubicon's offices, who will also conduct you to the site.

Your tender must be delivered to the architect's office, in the envelope provided, properly sealed, by not later than 12 noon on the 8th July 1969.

Yours faithfully,

SUTTON TO DRAUGHTSMAN

Dear Mr. Draughtsman, 10.6.69

LABWELS

The quantity surveyors have today distributed copies of the Bill of Quantities to the five firms we have agreed upon. Their tenders are due at this office not later than 12 noon on 8.7.69 (4 weeks from today). In my view they will need that length of time to make a proper job of pricing. In the meantime, I will, of course, be pressing on with detailed production drawings and other procedures which have to be done before the work really gets underway on site.

Could you please let me know whether you wish the tenders to be brought still sealed for opening in your presence, or whether I may open them here and report the results?

Yours sincerely,

DRAUGHTSMAN TO SUTTON

Dear Mr. Sutton, 12.6.69

LABWELS

When I got your letter saying that the builders were being given four weeks to tender in, I thought I should show it to Mr. Turvy, because we have never had to wait so long before when we had other architects working for us. He was a bit annoyed, because he has had one or two remarks about how long will it be before we see something on site and we have already had several delays, beyond what we regard as normal. He also thinks you should have consulted us before fixing the period.

We recently placed an order for a large concrete silo costing nearly half a million pounds and that tender was in after only two weeks.

I have my instructions to tell you to inform the builders that the period has been reduced to three weeks.

Yours faithfully,

Turvy seems to have conveniently forgotten that most of the delays so

"He always has two solutions to everything, and they are both good ones!"

far have been as a result of actions by Rubicon. This is a client's privilege. Being engineers, perhaps neither Turvy nor Draughtsman realise that pricing a Bill for a building is much more time-consuming, whatever the size, including as it does so many different trades and skills, than a thing like a concrete silo which an experienced contractor can probably price by just knowing its overall dimensions.

Whether or not Sutton fought this one we shall never know, but if so, he lost because we now see:

SUTTON TO FIVE BUILDERS

Dear Sirs, 14.6.69

Rubicon Ltd. LABWELS Building

I write to confirm my telephone message to the effect that my clients have instructed me to reduce the tendering period from four to three weeks, which means such tenders are now due at this office by 12 noon on 1.7.69. This was against my advice, but I have no option but to comply.

I confirm also that you will still be submitting a tender.

Yours faithfully,

We must hope Rubicon don't regret getting their prices in three weeks. It wasn't exactly tactful of Sutton to mention that the order was against his advice, but he probably wants to keep on good terms with the builders.

MRS. TURVY TO SUTTON

Dear Mr. Sutton, 21.6.69

I was so pleased to meet you and your charming wife at the Lockets' party last week. George has told me how impressed they are with you at Rubicon, and they are not easy to please. Someone, I can't remember who, said, 'He always has two solutions to everything, and they are both good ones.' Praise indeed!

I always particularly like this time of the year and when the weather is fine we usually have a few Sunday afternoon tennis parties. George says the court is in good condition now, so we are planning to have our 'first of the season' this coming Sunday – perhaps you both might like to come? It's likely you'll meet some other people you already know. There are usually a few spare rackets lying around, if that is a problem, but we do like people to wear white. I never think tennis looks right unless people do, do you?

Yours sincerely,

Dear God! "Topsy Turvy" – but what other name could she have after marrying a man called Turvy?

This letter heralds the start of a change in Sutton's relationship with Turvy from client to friend and he must be very pleased to know that Rubicon is corporately impressed. He also seems to have impressed Topsy. There is no further letter in the file, but we can assume they went, and in whites.

SUTTON TO DRAUGHTSMAN

Dear Mr. Draughtsman, 10.6.69

LABWELS Building

As agreed with you I opened the tenders received at 12 noon today in the presence of Mr. le Mesurier. There were only four because at the last moment Brickbat & Badger withdrew because they had not had sufficient time to complete their pricing. This is unfortunate because they were the firm you specifically asked to be included. The other four tenders are as follows:

Hovis Construction Ltd.	£108,755	52 weeks
Knott & Banister Ltd.	£109,646	52 weeks
Square, Kitchen & Co. Ltd.	£114,575	60 weeks
Truebuild Ltd.	£121,600	75 weeks

The figures are close enough to be called good competitive tendering except for Truebuild, who I suspect were not really trying. Hovis Construction, whilst not in the top size-bracket do work over a considerable area and have handled jobs of all sizes. As they are the lowest, I must recommend that their price is accepted.

I have called for their priced bill which must be checked by Cutt & Shuffle, before a contract is signed, and because of the narrow gap between the two lowest prices, I have also asked Knott & Banister for theirs. There is also nothing between them as regards time. I have in the past worked with both these firms. Knott & Banister are what we might call a regional firm who work within a thirty-mile radius of Winterfield and have handled projects a good deal larger than this one, so there is no doubt as their capacity. I believe you also have had experience of Hovis.

As soon as the checking has been completed, I will inform you of the result, and with your agreement will then draw up a contract on the RIBA standard form. I imagine the builder will require about a month to prepare before moving on to the site.

Yours sincerely,

As Sutton says, the prices all look genuine except for Truebuild who probably changed their minds about wanting the job when their tender period was cut by a week and pitched the figure well above what they expected the real cost to be.

When inviting quotations, employers do not bind themselves to accept 'the lowest or any tender', but they should do so, unless there are good reasons why not. A contractor passed over in this way is entitled to say, 'If you did not intend to give us the job, why ask us to tender in the first place'. A good question. There is a lot of work in pricing a Bill of Quantities all of which adds to the builder's overheads and plays its part in putting up building costs in general. The client, on the other hand might well say, 'The tender documents do not bind us to accept the lowest tender, and if we know the second lowest tenderer well we might wish to select him if the price difference is negligible or even small, but a considerable difference might incline us to accept the lowest price even from a firm we don't know.'

There is logic behind both points of view and the client might also say to the builder, reflecting his own approach to the situation, 'If you didn't like the conditions of contract, why did you tender?' Such treatment does nonetheless cause considerable bitterness in the building fraternity and is not liked by either architects or quantity surveyors, even though they may have the same feelings as the client. It is a fine and interesting point of moral judgement by the architect; for if he also thinks the second lowest firm would be likely to make a better job, should he not therefore recommend acceptance of that tender? Then again, although the architect is paid by, and only by *the client, he is nevertheless supposed to adjudicate impartially between client and builder (something which creates gusts of riotous laughter if mentioned at building federation meetings).*

RECORD OF TELEPHONE MESSAGE

Caller	James le Mesurier of Cutt & Shuffle
To	R.J.S.
Date	2.7.69. 11 a.m.
Job	LABWELS

Mr. le Mesurier rang re LABWELS. He says the Hovis Construction tender has a mistake. A complete page has been omitted when casting up, and this makes their real price £109,870 which is just above Knott & Bannister. He is checking their tender now. He also said that the Hovis Tender was overpriced in excavation and foundations. He is writing.

Betzy.

LE MESURIER TO SUTTON

Dear Richard,

LABWELS

You have doubtless seen my telephone message of yesterday. Since I made it I spoke to Hovis's estimator and he acknowledged the error. I explained that this put them in second place and the result was I received a call from their area manager, to the effect they would stick to their original offer. I don't suppose you will want that and I wouldn't recommend it. It complicates the measurement of site works, as prices will have to be revised and there is also another point at issue. I find the excavation and foundations are loaded, and as the underground services already there are not an entirely accurate forecast, there could be extras. I will let you know tomorrow about Knott & Banister.

Yours sincerely,

The only figure which means anything within the terms of the contract is the total which appears on the form of tender. The client could have cause for complaint at the builder being let off the hook. In this case, the error amounts to only about 1% which might not have presented much of a problem, but as a rule, nothing but trouble, even disaster, arises from forcing a builder to carry out a job which he has underpriced.

The practice of 'loading' the early site items is (or was) quite widespread. There are two reasons for this. These are the items which will form the basis of the first certificate (authority for payment) and also, foundations and excavation are parts of the work where variations are most likely to occur, since ground conditions must always be something of an unknown quantity. Even test bores at say 50 ft centres will not always disclose the full story.

The report on Knott & Banister must have been verbal and escaped recording (black mark Betzy). We now see:

SUTTON TO DRAUGHTSMAN

Dear Mr. Draughtsman, 4.7.69

LABWELS

I have now received le Mesurier's report on the two lowest tenders. It turns out that the lowest offer from Hovis Construction Ltd. contained an error as a page of the bill had been omitted when casting up the total. With this added, the total comes to £109,870. This is slightly above Knott & Banister's figure of £109,646 and I must therefore advise you to accept their offer. I have had a preliminary word with them and they ought to be able to take possession of the site in about four weeks' time.

Could you confirm that I am in order to instruct them?

Yours sincerely,

TURVY TO SUTTON

Dear Richard, 6.7.69

LABWELS Building

Leslie Draughtsman has consulted me about the tender situation. I would not hesitate to say that the advice we have had from you in the past has usually been sound, but in this present situation you do seem to be asking us to pay out more than we need without any obvious compelling reason. I know the difference is *only* a thousand pounds, but a thousand is a thousand especially in a contract where we have only £2,500 as contingency sum.

I would like to discuss it before you place any order.

Yours sincerely,

SUTTON TO KNOTT & BANISTER

Dear Sirs, 9.7.69

Rubicon Ltd. LABWELS Building

I am pleased to be able to inform you that my clients,

Rubicon Ltd. have authorised me to offer this contract to you on the basis of your tender dated 1.7.69 in the sum of £109,646.00. They wish you to move on to the site in the shortest possible time and I have informed them that you anticipate a date four weeks hence.

I am sending you herewith copies of drawings so far completed, particulars of sub-contractors and suppliers quotations, and my own draft programme for the job. Please contact Mr. le Mesurier of Cutt & Shuffle regarding the number of Bills of Quantities you will require for the administration of the project. I have already started on the preparation of contract documents and will let you know as soon as these are ready.

When you have had time to study these documents I would like to set up a meeting with yourselves, myself, my assistant who will be in charge of the detailed administration of the job, representatives of the client, and the quantity surveyor. I would suggest a week from today at 10.30 a.m. at this office. Please let me know immediately if this is convenient so that I can warn the other parties.

Yours faithfully,

Sutton is overdoing it. The meeting he envisages will have at least five people present, probably more, all of whom will want a say (otherwise why ask them?). It would have been better at this early stage to have an informal meeting with the representatives of the builder only, when they could have a friendly chat about the project in general and set about the job of establishing good relations. It has been truly said that the whole basis of success in the building industry is goodwill. Nothing can be built without it. We have noticed in the past a tendency in Sooty to over-formalise; he takes himself just a mite too seriously. There are others like this and all have a tendency to pontificate over contract management.

KNOTT & BANISTER TO SUTTON

Dear Sir, 10.7.69

Rubicon Ltd. LABWELS Building

We are obliged by your letter of yesterday's date and are pleased to have this opportunity of working under your direction. We acknowledge receipt of your drawings etc. and have spoken to Mr. le Mesurier about Bills.

Our Mr. Banister and Mr. Steele, who will be in charge of this project, will be pleased to attend your meeting on 16.7.69 to meet other persons who will be involved, but, with respect, might we also suggest a short informal meeting with just you and us. As builder and architect, we know we are the ones with most to do in getting this job underway and then through to completion. As we have not had the pleasure of working with you before, a preliminary discussion would be to mutual advantage. If you are agreeable we could wait on you at your office at, say, 11 a.m. on the 12th inst.

Yours faithfully,

Happily, there is a ring of sincerity about this letter and a feeling of genuine willingness to form and maintain good relations, which is by no means always the case. Knott & Banister is an old family firm, the Knott side having died out, and Sutton has been fortunate in the way the tenders have been settled.

Doubtless the meeting took place, but it was probably informal, since no notes appear to have been made.

9
Contracting and Expanding

WATT SPARK & CO. TO SUTTON

Dear Sir, 20.7.69

Rubicon Ltd. LABWELS Building

When we tendered for the electrical installation in this building we had no idea who the main contractor would be, but we were not overly concerned, getting on well with most. Now we find the main contractors are Knott & Banister we are most perturbed, because of bad experience in the past. Not to labour the matter unduly, on the contract we refer to we had great difficulty in getting our money, and never did get all of it.

We know that circumstances alter cases and so not to cause trouble, if it can be avoided, we will carry out the job providing we don't have to deal with a party called Scroggie. We have also to request that we are paid direct by Rubicon and not through Messrs. K. & B. seeing as we've had our whack of them.

We await your further instructions.

Yours faithfully,

This is a nasty one and somewhat of a surprise to Sutton, since the impression gained so far of Messrs. Knott & Banister has been favourable. There are firms who literally work on a shoe-string and hold off paying their sub-contractors in order to settle their previous months' debts. To have such a firm on a job is a real pain in the neck for any architect.

An architect can withhold payment of monies due to a sub-contractor and arrange for these to go direct, but it is both messy and undesirable. It affects the system of cash discounts and complicates the question of responsibility on the site. It is to be avoided if at all possible.

SUTTON TO KNOTT & BANISTER

Dear Sir, 21.7.69

Rubicon Ltd. LABWELS Building

I have heard from Watt Spark & Co. Ltd., the electrical contractors I have nominated, to the effect they are not willing to be appointed and paid by you. It seems there was some difficulty on a previous contract. They do say, however, that if they are appointed and paid directly by Rubicon they are willing to proceed. This is a situation I have met with once or twice in the past and it is not a method I approve of. The job of the main contractor, among other things, is to manage the whole operation on site, and the arrangement suggested above cuts across this procedure. Unfortunately, the price which Watt Spark have submitted is quite a lot lower than the next and I am unwilling to start incurring extras at this early stage. If therefore, you are agreeable to accepting them on your site, I will recommend my clients to accept this procedure.

Please let me know immediately.

Yours faithfully,

It would have been better to simply accept Watt Spark's resignation rather than risk further unpleasantness on site, but Sutton is tightly pinned down on costs and has left himself no room for manoeuvre. However, as he has heard no mention of the dubious 'Scroggie', he thinks there should be no real difficulties.

KNOTT & BANISTER TO SUTTON

Dear Sir, 22.7.69

Rubicon Ltd. LABWELS

Your letter of 21st inst. is to hand. Unfortunately, we are not surprised at the contents because we ourselves had some doubts about the involvement of Watt Spark & Co.

The trouble with this company blew up about three years ago on a job for Winterfield Borough Council. It was a tight programme and we needed maximum support from the subs. We didn't get it from Watt Spark who were a dilatory and unreliable lot of cowboys who let us down all along the line. They also seemed to get across our man Scroggie, who isn't one to let the grass grow under his feet. In the end we got caught on a time delay penalty and so we took some of it out on them. If they had tried at all we would have paid in full, but they must have known it was their fault because they never made any attempt to recover their losses.

On the other hand we believe that this may have been an isolated incident. They are a sizable firm usually considered reliable. Sometimes things can go sour, even when there is no good reason, so we are prepared to have another go and accept that they be paid direct.

This is also a good time to mention another difficulty of the same type. We are not at all happy about the nomination of Topps Roofers Ltd, and that's putting it mildly. Whenever we have had them in the past we have had trouble with a capital T, not only on site but afterwards. There have been more leaks than I've had hot dinners, and so about two years ago we decided never to use them again. I don't know how they keep going because they are always in money troubles, and screaming for a certificate before they've hardly started.

I'm sorry to have to say these things, but we feel sure that it is in your own and your client's interest to keep well away from these people. I wouldn't call them crooks, but they are not very far from it.

Yours faithfully,

Nominated sub-contractors, that is, those selected by the architect and not the builder himself, can be something of a problem and there is a school of thought which suggests they should be left out altogether and all subsidiary trades and skills be selected by the builder. This would have the advantage of leaving no doubt as to where the responsibility lies, in the event of defects arising. It would, however, considerably delay the preparation of the contract documents and getting the builder on site. The contractor has, of course, the right to refuse to appoint any particular sub. if he has good reason to do so.

SUTTON TO DRAUGHTSMAN

Dear Mr. Draughtsman, 23.7.69

LABWELS

We have a little problem with the electrical contractor. As you know we accepted a quotation from Watt, Spark & Co. who were one of the firms put forward by you. Unfortunately they have not been on good terms for some time with Knott & Banister because of something that happened on a previous contract. Watt Spark say they will only undertake the work if they are paid directly by you and not through Knott & Banister.

So far as I can see, there is no deep-seated mistrust between these two firms and Knott & Banister have agreed to accept this arrangement. Reading between the lines, I rather suspect they are both pleased to have the chance of repairing the rift. I do not anticipate any real problems and although the method of payment does slightly complicate the situation as regards responsibility on site, I think the risk is worth taking.

Could you please let me have your authority to proceed on these lines?

Yours sincerely,

Sooty would have been better off not mentioning that there was any risk to take. If things do go wrong he will no doubt be reminded of it. He has also forgotten to mention the roofing contractor.

DRAUGHTSMAN TO SUTTON

Dear Mr. Sutton, 25.7.69

LABWELS

I discussed the situation with Mr. Turvy and we definitely want Watt & Spark on the electrics. They have done a lot of work for us and all of it good. We agree to pay them direct.

Yours sincerely,

Short and to the point. Rubicon seem to have very definite views on the people who work for them and, anyway, are not very interested in the RIBA form of contract, which they themselves never use. This seems to get Sutton off the hook.

SUTTON TO KNOTT & BANISTER

Dear Sirs, 26.7.69

Rubicon Ltd. LABWELS Building

I now have authority from my client for you to appoint Watt, Spark & Co. for the electrical installation and they are to be paid directly by the client, so you will not need to include their work in interim certificate claims. Let us hope this contract will provide an opportunity for a reconciliation following the previous unhappy situation.

As regards Topps Roofers Ltd., it would be folly to appoint them in view of your past experiences. I am enclosing the quotation I received from Tarrag Ltd. and am writing to inform them they will be receiving your order. Being a firm of national standing, I cannot imagine there will be any objection to them.

On another subject, may I remind you I am still waiting for your detailed programme, which both my clients and I are anxious to see.

Yours faithfully,

SUTTON TO TOPPS ROOFING LTD.

Dear Sirs, 26.7.69

Rubicon Ltd. LABWELS Building

I am sorry to have to tell you that the main contractor for this building has now been appointed and is exercising his right, under the contract, not to accept the appointment of any particular nominated sub-contractor, in this case, you. I am sorry if this causes you any inconvenience, but there is nothing I can do to change the situation. You, of course, would have had the same right had you not been happy with the main contractor when appointed.

Yours faithfully,

There he goes again; always saying too much. A bald statement of facts would have been much better. Will he never learn?

TOPPS ROOFING LTD. TO SUTTON

Dear Sir, 28.7.69

Rubicon Ltd.

We acknowledge receipt of yours of 26.7.69 and are astonished at the contents. Are we right in our understanding that you wish to brush aside our firm contract to carry out the roofing on the above project? We would have you know that this formed a major part of our forward load, and that we have turned aside several other offers in order to oblige you in carrying it out.

Having looked into the matter with a legal man, we must inform you it is not our intention to take it lying down. We have your 'letter of intent' to place an order when the main contractor was appointed and we assumed it meant what it said, i.e. that an order would be placed as soon as a contractor was selected. On this basis we have gone ahead, ordered materials and reserved space in our programme of work to fit it in. Having gone to these lengths we feel justified in expecting you to keep to your side of the bargain as agreed. Bearing in mind that we are a firm of repute, we must insist that you put matters right and instruct Knott & Banister to place their order with us forthwith.

Yours faithfully,

A letter which no firm of good repute would have written. Topps Roofing must be really desperate to take a line like this, and must imagine that Sutton is very naive to be influenced by such a tirade. Although 'Sooty' may have some misgivings, he handles the matter with a sang-froid which would have done justice to an older man. We gain the impression that Sutton's forte is unflappability, a very useful asset.

SUTTON TO TOPPS ROOFING LTD.

Dear Sirs, 31.7.69

Rubicon Ltd.

I acknowledge your letter of 28.7.69 and have never read such a farrago of nonsense in my whole career. As you very well know, a letter of intent does not constitute a contract. It is, as the name implies, a statement of an intention to proceed, in due course, with the proposals which form the basis of the installation described. It does not constitute a contract, otherwise what would be the point of using such a device in the first place? Firms who accept such instructions do so on the understanding that an order will most likely follow, but this is not guaranteed.

I am sorry that you feel aggrieved, but Knott & Banister have now placed their order with the firm next below you on the tender list.

Yours faithfully,

A confident letter indeed, but is it also competent? It would certainly frighten off some not-too-bright tradesman, but Topps Roofers are not in that class. Whether he knows it or not, the situation is not quite as Sutton makes out. He cannot go merrily along making promises in his client's name and then simply refute them later. A letter of intent does commit his client to paying for any material obtained and any work done in preparation for this particular project. He may be bluffing, in which case his bluff is now called:

TOPPS ROOFING LTD. TO SUTTON

Dear Sir, 2.8.69

Rubicon LABWELS

We acknowledge receipt of yours of 31.7.69 and are sorry to note that you do not intend to give us satisfaction in this matter. As you have stated it is not your intention to honour your side of the bargain for the above project, we have been forced to have the matter looked into again and find, as we first surmised, that your understanding of contract law is lacking as regards your present financial obligations to us.

We are given to understand that we are entitled to be paid for any work done and any materials ordered for this job. By our reckoning this amounts to nearly £2,000 and we intend to sue for it.

Yours faithfully,

SUTTON TO TOPPS ROOFING LTD.

Dear Sirs, 3.8.69

Rubicon LABWELS

Let me have details of the claim you intend to make. This letter does not imply acceptance of any liability on behalf of my client.

Yours faithfully,

At last Sutton has discovered the virtues of brevity. I suspect he has sought advice from a more experienced colleague, McDonald perhaps.

There is little wonder Topps Roofing are not popular. It is amazing they have any clients left at all. Unfortunately, they probably have no goodwill left and nothing to lose by being offensive.

SUTTON TO LE MESURIER

Dear James, 6.8.69

LABWELS Building

I have a tricky little situation on my hands with Topps Roofing. Knott & Banister have positively refused to have them on site, and from the tone of their letters I am not surprised. We can all do without people like that. I enclose copies of the correspondence so far. I also enclose their priced list of labour and material which they claim are attributable to this job.

Would you let me have your opinion on the validity of the claim and the prices?

Yours sincerely,

A nice thing about quantity surveyors is that they can and do form a valuable ally when trouble strikes. An architect can feel very lonely without them. James le Mesurier is a very good example of the helpful QS because on this occasion, he not only tenders advice, but agrees to take the matter off Sooty's hands altogether as we see from the following copy letter:

CUTT & SHUFFLE TO TOPPS ROOFING

Dear Sirs, 9.8.69

Rubicon LABWELS Building

R. J. Sutton, the architect for this building, has passed us your claim for labour and materials, which you say have been expended to date on this project, your authority being the architect's letter of intent. We have the following observations:

1. We consider that the rates you have used are too high if they are intended, as they should be, to be the same as those used in preparing your tender.

2. The labour content is excessive since all it can really represent is unloading and storage of materials.

3. Apart from the white marble chippings, which are perhaps

a bit special, the whole of the material can be used on other jobs and we fail to see how you can claim it was obtained specifically for this job.

We have therefore recommended the architect to accept responsibility for the chippings and he will arrange to have them collected as soon as site space and transport are available. Payment will be made by the contractor.

In our view this is the limit of Rubicon's responsibility to you and there is no point in pursuing the matter further.

Yours faithfully,

cc R. J. Sutton

LE MESURIER TO SUTTON

Dear Richard, 9.8.69

I enclose a copy of my letter to Topps Roofing. I think this meets the case and we ought not to hear anything further from them. If they do continue to bleat; I suggest we just ignore it. I take it you will get either K & B or Tarrag to collect the chippings. As we are virtually losing nothing I see no reason for us to bring Rubicon into the matter at all.

Yours sincerely,

Well done le Mesurier who has extracted Sutton from the mess very neatly. Topps Roofing, however, cannot resist one last swipe:

TOPPS ROOFING TO SUTTON

Dear Sir,

We acknowledge a letter of 9.8.69 sent at your instigation by James le Mesurier of Cutt & Shuffle. Now we have been fully apprised as to the standards of conduct of the people we have been dealing with, we have been advised that our best course is to let the matter drop legally, but to take such steps as may be necessary to protect other honest tradesmen from similar dealings with you and your kind. Our numerous friends in the trade will shortly therefore be hearing about this and we would be obliged if both you and Cutt & Shuffle would send no further enquiries. You need not trouble yourselves about the chippings, as we will doubtless find another use for them.

There is no subscription, just 'Topps Roofing' who really ought to be a bit more careful. There is a touch of libel in the first paragraph and a hint of blackmail in the second. If Sutton turns nasty they could regret this letter. As it is he chooses to ignore it. It is most unlikely that Topps will have 'numerous friends in the trade'.

10

'Bomber' Takes the Chair

KNOTT & BANISTER TO SUTTON

Dear Sir, 8.8.69

Rubicon LABWELS

In accordance with your request we have today taken possession of the site for the above project and have now commenced erecting site huts. We hope a lot of progress will not be anticipated for a week or two because our trench digger has been delayed on another job and, as you know, the site is criss-crossed with all kinds of underground services, which will require a lot of hand digging when we get down a bit. A clerk of works has now appeared on site and has impressed upon us the importance of not damaging any part of the network of services, which we understand are pretty thick underground. His name is Mr. Reg. Harris, but around the sites he is known as 'Bomber' Harris. I understand he has yet to meet you although he is employed direct by Rubicon. He has a reputation of being a real stickler, but he is fair and we think we will get on with him.

Yours faithfully,

SUTTON TO DRAUGHTSMAN

Dear Mr. Draughtsman, 9.8.69

LABWELS Building

As you know, the builder has taken possession of the site and is erecting his cabins etc. I understand you have appointed one of your own staff as clerk of works, a Mr. Harris. Since clerks of works are supposed to work under the direction of the architect, it would obviously be desirable if I met him straight away. Could you arrange this please? I am free any day this week, except Thursday.

Yours sincerely,

Sooty sounds a bit piqued. The RIBA Conditions of Engagement state, 'The clerk of works shall be nominated and directed by the architect and appointed and paid by the client' but not all employers are happy with this situation, and tend to see the COW as their own watchdog not only on the builder, but also on the architect, who is frequently regarded as concerned only with his art and not much use when faced with the harsh realities of the site.

In Rubicon's case this is even more so, because Harris is their own man who superintends all construction work, of which the work designed by architects forms only a small proportion. Once again Sutton looks like making Draughtsman's hackles rise by standing on his dignity.

TURVY TO SUTTON

Dear Richard, 11.8.69

Leslie Draughtsman seems a bit put out by a recent letter from you concerning his appointment of 'Bomber' Harris. I must say I am not surprised. I don't know why it is that you and Draughtsman don't hit it off. Leslie may seem a bit prickly at times, but this is understandable as he sees you as poaching on his preserves. He is, however, a good chap and intensely loyal to the Company which he has served for 15 years. I had hoped that by now you would be working happily together. I think only a small gesture would be needed to break the ice but it would have to come from you and I hope I can rely on you to make it.

Turning now to the question of Harris, the sort of situation which you envisage, and which is no doubt normal on other contracts, cannot really apply here. Harris is not just a clerk of works – in fact we call him a site engineer, and I regard him as a senior member of my staff. He graduated from the tools to become a foreman and subsequently to his present status. Consequently he is a stickler for good workmanship which is no bad thing these days. He is also renowned for his extensive vocabulary of Anglo-Saxon words, which he uses to good effect at site meetings, which he normally chairs. I know there is more than one opinion about who should take the chair at these meetings, but this arrangement has worked well for us in the past and I would not like to change it now.

Could you come along to my office on Friday at 2.20 p.m. and I will introduce you?

Yours sincerely,

It seems that Sooty is going to have to toe the line on this one no matter how much his pride is hurt. As Turvy says, there is more than one opinion on who should chair site meetings. Most, but not all, architects prefer to take the chair themselves on the understanding that the architect is 'leader of the building team'. Some, however, hold the view that the site is the province of the builder and he should have charge of everything that happens there. Rubicon, as a firm with a large and continuing volume of construction work, prefer to have their own man, sometimes to the discomfort of both the architect and the builder.

SUTTON TO TURVY

Dear George, 12.8.69

Thank you for your letter. I can see that Leslie Draughtsman has no reason to regard me kindly and I will see what can be done to improve the atmosphere. It is most important that we should work well together, and I am grateful to you for being tactful enough to point it out.

On the question of the clerk of works I must admit to a lack of experience. The work I have done so far in my capacity as a private practitioner, has not been of sufficient size to merit the appointment of a clerk of works. I have naturally had jobs where one has been present, but this was when I was on the staff of Leverpullers. My instinct tells me that the right way to work is the way the RIBA direct, but I cannot give a logical explanation why. In any case, if you as my employer decide that you wish to appoint your own COW, I cannot demur.

I therefore accept your proposals and look forward to meeting the redoubtable Mr. Harris on Friday in your office.

Yours sincerely,

SUTTON TO DRAUGHTSMAN

Dear Mr. Draughtsman, 16.8.69

I expect Mr. Turvy has told you that I met Mr. Harris in

his office last Friday and that we established the arrangement that is to prevail concerning our various responsibilities.

It has been agreed that in addition to the normal duties of a clerk of works, he will be chairing the site meetings, and will have with you the responsibility of watching over your employers' interests during the execution of the works on site. Although this is not the usual way of doing things under the RIBA form of contract, I can see no reason why it should not work well. Mr. Turvy has left it to you and me to work out the details of an arrangement to ensure there is no cross-traffic or duplication of effort. I shall look forward to discussing this with you at the first available opportunity and in any case before the work on site advances beyond the present preliminary stage.

Yours sincerely,

Sutton is doing his level best to break the ice as Turvy has requested and this letter will go a long way towards doing just that. As we have noted before, Sooty can write a good tactful letter when he wishes. He has really been trying here and we need not doubt his sincerity.

11

Shifting Sands

KNOTT & BANISTER TO SUTTON

Dear Sir, 14.8.69

Rubicon LABWELS

This to formally advise you that we have made a proper start on the excavation this week and that we have already run into trouble. According to the bill we priced, the ground should be good 2-ton clay and some of it is, but unfortunately not all. In the north-west corner we ran into running sand and this seems to extend over about a quarter of the site. We have had this before in the Winterfield area and it can be quite a problem which has meant either short piles, sheet piling or de-watering equipment. Mr. Harris has seen it and says we are to get your instructions straight away. In the meantime, he is discussing it with Mr. Draughtsman.

We shall be pleased to have your comments and instructions as soon as possible.

Yours faithfully,

This is rather a nasty one. The reader will remember there was no site investigation, Sutton accepting Turvy's advice that there were no problems as regards the subsoil, only with the underground services. It now appears that not only was this not so, but as these conditions have been found elsewhere in Winterfield, something of the sort might have been anticipated.

For the technically minded, short piles would seek to overcome the problem by going down far enough through the sand to reach good firm ground below; sheet piles are driven down interlocking with each other so as to form a continuous barrier around the excavated area to hold back the sand until the excavation is complete; dewatering equipment is a series of perforated tubes driven into the ground around the perimeter of the area to be excavated, which are then connected to each other and then to a pump which lowers the level of the water in the ground, enabling the sand to dry out and thus become stable. An architect of Sutton's limited experience might not be acquainted with this process.

The interesting thing about running sand is that it is only unstable when it is not confined. When it is confined, it has a very good load-bearing capacity and is only a problem during excavation. Once the foundations are laid and the trenches back-filled it is quite stable.

The reference to 2-ton clay is the builder's way of saying that the ground can take a safe load of 2 tons per ft^2. (Today that would be 20 tonnes per m^2.)

SUTTON TO TURVY

Dear George, 15.8.69

Forgive me for breaking the rules on this occasion by writing directly to you. This is only because it is a matter of some seriousness which Leslie Draughtsman would have had to consult you on in any case; indeed, I have no doubt he already has.

During the progress of the excavations, K & B have come across an area of running sand which neither you nor I had anticipated. This is not a disaster, but it may well result in a significant delay. There is more than one way of dealing with the problem and Leslie Draughtsman is discussing the possibilities with Bomber Harris, who between them have considerably more experience than I have of this type of foundation problem. My own instinct, however, tells me that the most promising solution and the one which will cause the least delay, is to use piles in the area of running sand. This way no excavation is needed, and I think I know a firm who would be able to move in and start at very short notice.

The firm I have in mind is called Uriah Heap Ltd. They were particularly persona grata at Leverpullers and I dare say you also know them. Their system involves the use of lining tubes so there is no difficulty in operating through running sand.

I will not do anything, of course, without your authority, but if I have that, I am sure we could have them on site taking test bores within a week, and not much later for the actual job. Dewatering is a long job and sheet piling a bit uncertain without knowng the exact extent and depth of the sand.

Yours sincerely,

Sutton is jumping in feet first. He can know only a very little about soil mechanics, which is a highly specialised part of building design for which the architect, who has to be Jack of all trades and master of none, has to rely on the advice of specialists. He would have been wiser to take a few more days and call in an independent expert to advise on the choice of method. True, the piling contractor is going to do some test bores, but he is obviously going to recommend piling.

Sutton should also have borne in mind that he has not got a lay client on this occasion, as Rubicon has civil engineers within its own ranks who are, or should be, expert in foundation design. If it had not been for this he might well have made his own decision and instructed Uriah Heap Ltd. without even consulting his client. He is, after all, being paid to take decisions, but in this case his wisest choice would have been to seek his client's wishes without even offering an opinion.

At the start of his second paragraph, Sutton is quietly reminding Turvy that they should share the blame, if blame there be, for this episode.

TURVY TO SUTTON

Dear Richard, 18.8.69

LABWELS Foundations

This is to confirm the decisions taken when we met on site

earlier today, together with Draughtsman, Harris and Banister and Steele from the builder's office.

Having discussed the three most likely ways of meeting the problem, there was a divergence of opinion, the builder's people, yourself and Harris going for loadbearing piles, whereas Draughtsman and I were in favour of using sheet piling and normal foundations. Not only was this a four to two majority, but it was those who actually have the job of getting this building out of the ground who favoured piles. A firm decision to do this was therefore made, and I am now confirming it.

It was also agreed that you should instruct U. Heap Ltd. to get on with test bores as soon as possible, if not earlier. I do hope this will have as little effect on the programme as you seem to think.

Yours sincerely,

This looks like a very neat example of 'passing the buck'. If all goes well he and Draughtsman take their share of the credit, if not, he has disassociated himself from the decision taken. To be fair, however, Turvy is not a man to shirk responsibility and would accept that this was a joint decision. We shall see!

SUTTON TO URIAH HEAP LTD.

Dear Sirs, 20.8.69

Rubicon Ltd. LABWELS Building

This is to confirm my telephone call earlier today to the effect that you are to carry out a ground investigation by the use of trial bores over part of the site of the above building where running sand has been encountered. The number and depth of the bores required is a matter for you to decide.

I understand you are in a position to move one or more test rigs on to the site on Monday next, and that by the end of the week you would anticipate having enough information to allow a scheme to be put forward for a piled foundation.

Time here is of the utmost importance. Both the client and the builder are very anxious that time delays are kept to an absolute minimum, the former because their present welfare facilities are woefully inadequate, and the latter because, in building, time is money.

I look forward to having your report at the earliest.

Yours faithfully,

The earliest what? This is is business jargon and not worthy of Sutton. Perhaps he is just worried. True, the situation does demand speed, but Sutton doesn't have to keep repeating it, or keep on explaining why to a firm which cannot really wish to know. They've already said that they can get on with it and that should be good enough. A little more of the 'Drake on Plymouth Ho' attitude would be more appropriate.

There is another aspect of time problem. If a firm comes in at a moment's notice, to get someone out of trouble, possibly putting off other things, they are going to charge more than the going rate. The more obvious it is that the employer is desperate, the more they are going to charge. There is always an optimum rate of work for any job and to move either way from this norm is inevitably to increase costs.

URIAH HEAP LTD. TO SUTTON

Daer Sir, 28.8.69

Rubicon Ltd.

As agreed we have done a total of six test-bores and find that the depth of the running sand varies considerably even on this small area, from a few feet up to 50 in one corner. The strata below the sand also varies but there is good boulder clay just below, it seems over the whole area.

We suggest we use our standard 15″ bored piles going down about 5′ into the clay at approx. 10′ centres. We shall have to tube all the way because of the sand and the tubes left in. From the drawings you supplied we estimate this will give you adequate load-bearing capacity for the building as designed, plus a future storey should this ever be needed.

Fortunately, we have just called in two rigs from another job and could move them up to your site next week. We expect, if no snags are encountered, we could complete in four weeks.

We await your further instructions with interest.

Yours faithfully,

SUTTON TO KNOTT & BANISTER

Dear Sirs, 29.8.69

LABWELS Building

Uriah Heap Ltd. have been appointed to place piles for foundations at the north side of the site and will be bringing in two piling rigs next Monday. You are requested to give them all necessary assistance in getting their rigs set up, supplying water and power and disposing of waste to tip.

They anticipate completing their task in four weeks leaving all ready for the construction of the pile beams which will form the foundations over that part of the site. I have arranged for the design of these beams to be carried out by the Corkscrew Bar Co. Ltd., who will also supply the reinforcement and fix it, as they are already doing for the normal loadbearing foundations on the rest of the site. As soon as I receive their quotation I will require you to place your official order, which will be in replacement for part of the material and labour in their original quotation which will not now be required.

Both my clients and I are concerned that this unfortunate episode should cause as little delay as possible. Now that the extent of the problem is known, you should plan to take whatever steps are possible to keep the delay to the minimum. For instance there is no reason why the foundations over the two-thirds of the site not affected, should not proceed normally whilst the piling rigs are on site, and preparations can be made to see that the formwork for the pile beams comes on site ready for fixing as soon as there are some completed pile caps to connect. Drawings detailing the beam reinforcement and formwork should be in your hands within three days.

If these steps are taken, I can see no reason why the total delay should exceed three weeks, but I would like to have your opinion on this together with your programme, revised to take account of these developments.

Yours faithfully,

No doubt he would, but he is unlikely to get it until Knott & Banister Ltd. have the piling contractor on site and some opportunity to see how he is progressing. In this kind of situation the builders are as old as Methuselah compared with Sooty's bright young tiger approach. They will certainly amend their programme in due course but not until they see how the 'cookie crumbles'.

KNOTT & BANISTER TO SUTTON

Dear Sir, 31.8.69

Rubicon LABWELS

We have your letter regarding the piling and will make all necessary provisions for Uriah Heap Ltd. We have had them on our site before now and they have usually done well, but they are going to have to pedal hard if they are to complete in four weeks with two rigs. A lot will depend on the weather.

We note your comments about keeping going on the rest of the site, but with due respect, it is not as easy as you make it sound. The site is very restricted. In fact, there is no space whatever for a compound, which means we have no space outside the site for materials etc. It was difficult enough without having pilers on the site at the same time. However, we will see what can be done.

Yours faithfully,

K & B Ltd. are reacting exactly as one might expect from a firm with their background. The letter is a cautious one but shows a willingness to try without committing themselves. Sutton can expect no more.

It seems he has given his instructions to the Corkscrew Bar Co. Ltd. verbally, because we next read:

THE CORKSCREW BAR CO. LTD. TO SUTTON

Dear Sir, 31.8.69

Rubicon Ltd. Winterfield

We thank you for your revised instructions and as requested have redesigned the foundations over that part of the site where piles are now being used. Unfortunately, because of the overturning moment engendered by the long span beams at two points on the perimeter, the arrangement of piles suggested by Heaps will not do and at least four raking piles will be required. The alternative would be to use much larger piles at these points, but we are of the opinion that this would be more expensive.

The changes will involve removing some of the already bent steel from the site and replacing it with new, but providing the main and piling contractors can move quickly, we should not add to the delay you have already incurred, although there will, naturally, be some extra cost.

We await your further instructions.

Yours faithfully,

NOTES OF A SITE MEETING HELD AT THE OFFICES OF RUBICON LTD. AT 11 A.M. ON 3.9.69

The principal business of the meeting was to deal with the current state of the work on site and was primarily concerned with the foundation problems at present being encountered. Apart from the client's reps. and us the principal attenders were K & B Ltd., U.H. Ltd., and Corkscrew Bars. The discussion centred on the need to provide raking piles. U.H. have the capacity to provide these, but a special rig is needed and they will not have one available until next week. Bomber's comment, which one realised subsequently was typical, was, 'Right, you better find a ******** ***** ***** you can get here this ******** week'. This didn't produce quite the reaction one might expect and it became apparent that this was not the first time that the rep. from U.H. had met the 'Bomber'. The upshot was a compromise that the rig was to be moved over the weekend (at double time of course) so as to be ready for work on the Monday morning. This was probably what U.H. had intended all the time, but knowing the Bomber had kept a little back to bargain with. Corkscrew Bars confirmed they could tie in with these arrangements and all was sweetness and light.

Several other sub-contractors attented principally to make their faces known and take home messages to their employers as to how and when they were expected to perform. (If I say I want you on the site on the 10th, I mean the * * * * * * * * tenth and not the * * * * 20th or even the * * * * 15th and I want you with all your * * * * equipment and materials. * * * * bodies alone are no * * * * good to me. I'm a good man to work for if you keep your * * * * noses * * * * clean, but I can turn * * * * nasty if you're not * * * * careful.)

K & B's programme was put up for all to study and comment on and Bomber announced that from that day forward it was to be his Bible and it had * * * * well better be everyone elses.

The meeting broke up in a somewhat subdued atmosphere. I was promised a copy of Bomber's official minutes and cannot wait to read them.

Sooty has clearly been both astonished and intrigued by his first experience of Harris in action. We know he started on the tools, but one cannot help but feel that a sometime or other he must have been in the Army and rose at least to the rank of full Sergeant. The likeliest thing is that he joined the Royal Engineers, where he could have received both military and trade training. The fact that Bomber includes shorthand among his many gifts is just as well, given the tone of his meetings.

One would have thought that such scant regard for his status would have put Sutton on his dignity, but one feels that he was left gasping for breath. He cannot leave it like that, however, and will have to assert his authority before long. This is bound to be interesting and instructive. Steele of K & B should also see he is not pushed around as the site has been 'handed over' and is now in his charge. Not even the employer has the right to do as he pleases there.

KNOTT & BANISTER TO SUTTON

Dear Sir, 30.9.69

LABWELS Rubicon

Corkscrew Bars left the site today after finishing the fixing. Uriah Heap finished three days ago and we are now ready to cast the pile beams. Bluepath Grey have supplied us with their foundation bolts for casting in and we expect them on site next week.

Cutt and Shuffle have had a young man here for the past few days (not Mr. le Mesurier) and he has been measuring with our agent's QS the alterations arising out of the foundation problems. We hope that sees the end of it.

Yours faithfully,

And no doubt so does Sutton. Please, dear reader, do not think all building contracts have as many problems as this one. After all, we are hardly yet out of the ground. I suspect, however, this job has a gremlin and we haven't seen the last of him yet.

On jobs of this size it is normal for the two quantity surveyors representing the employer and the builder respectively to measure vari-

*"I'm a good man to work for if you keep your * * * * * * * noses clean, but I can turn * * * * * * * nasty if you don't."*

ations on the site as they occur. The value of any extras can then be included in the interim certificates (which are issued monthly) and the builder does not have to wait until the end of the contract for payment.

12

Lunches and Lurches

LE MESURIER TO SUTTON

Dear Richard, 15.8.69

LABWELS Rubicon

Our senior partner, Norman Cutt, is paying one of his routine visits to this office next week. One item of business he will wish to deal with is our fee account for the work done so far, and he has also expressed a wish to meet you, this being the first job we have done together in your capacity as a private practitioner.

If you are agreeable, we could attend on you at your office at around twelve on Wednesday next week and go on from there to lunch at Groucho's which is new but got a good report in Egon Ronay recently. We can surely allow ourselves a little relaxation occasionally even if it does tend to spoil the afternoon's work.

Yours,

Dear me! this doesn't sound like James le Mesurier who has so far not put a foot wrong. We know that his business contacts with Sutton are on a friendly basis, but this is presuming too far. Whether or not Sooty can allow himself to relax at midday is his affair and only his. The only explanation seems to be that he was slightly tipsy when he wrote it, something to be avoided like the plague.

SUTTON TO LE MESURIER

Dear James, 16.8.69

Thank you for your letter and the invitation to lunch extended on behalf of your senior partner. I shall of course, be pleased to meet him and discuss any matters concerning the LABWELS project, although I would have thought that all such matters could be safely left to you.

As you know, I am not a great one for business lunches which, as you rightly observe, tend to shorten the working day by a disproportionate amount. But we all have to eat, so if you wish I will be happy to join you at some simple hostelry, but perhaps not Groucho's on this occasion.

Yours sincerely,

We get the feeling that our Sooty is something of an ascetic and probably only eats lunch every other day. Reading between the lines, it could just be that Sutton suspects Cutt's motives in wanting to meet him.

SUTTON TO McDONALD (PERSONAL)

Dear Ian, 21.8.69

I think I told you I appointed Cutt & Shuffle as QSs for the Rubicon job. James le Mesurier, who is handling this job, is an excellent QS and a good chap into the bargain.

Yesterday I was invited to meet Cutt, their senior partner, who is based somewhere near Regent's Park, and to join him for lunch at that very expensive new restaurant called 'Groucho's'. I was glad I managed to settle for a hamburger because I found him positively nauseating. What is more to the point, he seemed to be dropping rather blatant hints concerning further work he has heard I am to have from Rubicon. I have no idea of the source of this information, but if it is true, naturally I shall be very pleased. Cutt, however, wants to make sure he gets in on it and suggested there could be something in it for me, in the shape of a percentage of their fees. I was completely non-commital and I expect he went his way under the impression that I am thinking it over.

The thing is, what am I to do about it? You know how I loathe this kind of thing and I feel I should either report it direct to his own Institute or to the RIBA and let them decide what, if anything, should be done. The difficulty is there were no witnesses, as he was careful not to raise the subject when le Mesurier was near. No doubt that is his usual procedure.

I would greatly welcome your advice. I don't want to embarrass le Mesurier, who, as I said, is a good guy. Perhaps I should just drop it and try to avoid meeting the wretched twit again.

Yours,

Although this is a dreadful state of affairs, the reader should not infer that such practices are widespread. On the contrary, they are very rare indeed, and also very difficult to prove. No Discipline Committee can take action unless the persons involved are prepared to go before them and give evidence at first hand or swear out an affidavit. Not unnaturally, most people are reluctant to go to these lengths, and are inclined to forget it for the sake of peace and quiet. This is why the few bent professionals who adopt such methods seem to get away with it, at least for some time. Sutton is turning again to his friend and benefactor, McDonald for advice based on a longer experience than his own.

SUTTON TO LE MESURIER

Dear James, 22.8.69

I have your firm's fee account for the work up to pre-contract stage. As you know, I suggested to Rubicon they should deal with you direct as regards your fees, but they have requested that they should come via this office. This being so, I have a duty to study them and make any relevant comments.

I find that, as I would expect, they are strictly in accordance with your Institute's scales, but there is an item which I am sure will raise some eyebrows at Rubicon who are good payers, but who don't like to be overcharged any more than the next man. The item I refer to is the charge for printing and lithography. You must surely be able to get an awful lot of copies for £250 and as we only invited five tenders it is hard for me to offer any explanation. There are, I know, copies needed for the contract, the site, myself etc., but surely not to that extent.

I thought you would like a chance to reconsider this item before I forward the account to the client.

Yours,

This is a friendly gesture on Sutton's part. He could have just forwarded the account to Rubicon and waited for the screams of anguish to arise. As it seems likely the account has been prepared by Cutt, he must have been tempted to do just that. However, he likes le Mesurier and wants to deal fairly with him.

McDONALD TO SUTTON (STRICTLY PRIVATE)

Dear Sooty, 23.8.69

I have your letter about Cutt and it certainly seems you have

"He seemed to be dropping rather blatant hints."

a problem on your hands. I have never met a bent QS, or other consultant for that matter, but I have met a lot who blatantly break their own code by making unsolicited approaches for commissions without any sign of embarrassment whatever. There have also been those who have tried to push Christmas presents at me. One expects that sort of thing from builders, but not from professionals. Of course, I have never been in private practice, where the code of ethics has to be much more in evidence. There are parts which don't apply to those of us who are salaried, so perhaps I am not the best person to advise you. Nevertheless, I will try.

Putting myself in your shoes, I would be inclined to report the matter. Not to do so would be a dereliction of the duty you owe to your fellow architects and I would go first to the RIBA, preferably in person. I expect you have reason to visit London occasionally and next time you could just drop in and have an informal chat. The man to see is David Blore.

As regards the situation with Condorco, you must be quite chuffed to hear you may be getting another job from them. I have no idea as to where Cutt could have got his information, but I expect it will be correct. People like him don't often make mistakes. In view of what has happened, you will obviously have to think twice about employing those people again. It seems hard on le Mesurier though, who has so far served you well. I think you will just have to wait and see how things go, but do let me know what Blore says about Cutt.

Yours,

LE MESURIER TO SUTTON

Dear Richard, 25.8.69

LABWELS Fees

Thank you for your letter. The cost of printing the bills reflects our policy of trying to make them, or at least a few of them, 'objets d'art!' You architects take great pride in your drawings, and even those which are intended only for the site have a good deal of unnecessary time lavished on them, because the draughtsman is proud of his skill and cannot produce a shoddy drawing to save his life.

We also like to feel we have some usually pleasing record of our work and we therefore go in for some very elegant and expensive printing and binding for a few special copies for client, architect, builder and for our own library copy. You will be receiving one soon. I admit we do not seek authority for doing this at the employer's expense, and if you wish, I think I could talk Mr. Cutt into charging only for the standard copies, although he is a keen one for getting his 'pound of flesh'.

By the way, the partner in charge of this office, T. A. B. Smythe, visits once a week and would like to meet you. There are one or two things he would like to discuss with you. Would 3 p.m. next Wednesday suit you, either at your office or here?

Yours sincerely,

Who would have suspected the soul of an artist within those stern, unbending minds? But unfortunately, they are gratifying their artistic longings at the client's expense. As James is careful to point out, however, architects do this all the time by spending more time than is strictly necessary on drawings only needed for construction. The draughtsman sees the drawing as an end in itself, not just a means to an end and no one is going to persuade him otherwise. This is, however, at the architect's own expense, since his fees are not controlled by the time spent on his drawings.

le Mesurier's reference to Cutt's pound of flesh won't endear him to his senior partner should he ever read it, but even if copies of all correspondence go through normally to head office, as with some firms they do, he could arrange to avoid that in this case.

SUTTON TO LE MESURIER

Dear James, 25.8.66

LABWELS

I read your letter with interest and look forward to receiving the special presentation copy of your Bill for this job. However, I am afraid I can't ask my client to pay for this small extravagance and would therefore request you to revise your account to include only the normal print-out. If you will then re-submit it, I will see it is presented without further delay.

Yours sincerely,

TURVY TO SUTTON

Dear Richard, 25.8.69

On this occasion I am not concerned with LABWELS but with another project which may be of interest to you.

As you are probably aware, the expansion of Rubicon's manufacturing capability, which seems certain to continue, means a corresponding expansion of management and staff. With this in mind we have just concluded arrangements to purchase some more land which, although not immediately adjacent to our present site, is near enough not to matter. Our proposals for plant erection on this site are not yet final, but we do know we are going to need office space for an additional 200 staff at least.

Although I do not yet have the Board's authority to appoint an architect, I shall be recommending you when the time comes and I hope you will be able to take it on. In the meantime, I would like to discuss it with you. Leslie Draughtsman and his boys have been looking into the possibilities in a very preliminary way, but have already come up with some proposals, giving an indication of the size and cost of the new building. Would Wednesday suit you at, say, 11.30 a.m.? Do stay to lunch if you wish as our Chairman will be present and he has expressed a desire to meet you.

Yours sincerely,

This is the best news Sooty could have had as it means he is becoming established. The biggest worry a young architect has during the early years of his practice is the supply of commissions to keep him going. Since his code of practice forbids him to tout for work (an unpleasant word to use for making unsolicited approaches to possible clients, which is common practice for firms in normal commercial situations) he must wait for the approach to come from the client. Real security can be achieved only through the establishment of good relations with clients who have a continuing need for building development, such as Local Authorities or large industrial corporations.

The meeting probably took place but we hear no more about it, because the new job has doubtless been consigned to a new file.

SUTTON TO McDONALD

Dear Ian, 30.8.69

The most appalling thing has happened which, despite your good advice, will probably resolve that worrying business with Norman Cutt.

I had a 'phone call from John le Mesurier yesterday and he

told me that friend Cutt apparently had one good business lunch too many because two or three days after seeing me he wrapped himself and some luckless client round a tree. They are both in a coma in Charing Cross Hospital. Apparently, Cutt's wife has been told he'll pull through, but his passenger, who went straight through the windscreen, may not be so lucky. Whatever happens, Cutt is plainly going to be out of action for quite a while and in the circumstances, I think it would be decent to let the matter drop. The only good thing to emerge is that if Cutt is off the scene for a lengthy period, le Mesurier might be in line for partnership, so it's an ill wind etc.

I'm sorry Sue and I will not be able to come over for dinner on Sunday next. There's nothing I'd like better, but we're already engaged to go to the Turvy's for a tennis and Coq au Vin marathon. However, thanks again for the invitation and I do hope we'll be able to meet for a drink soon.

Yours,

13
Plots and Pans

MRS. BEETON TO SUTTON

Dear Mr. Sutton, 20.8.69

I know it is early days yet, but the kitchen equipment contractors, Bains Marie Ltd. have approached me about getting our lay-out sorted out, because they need a lot of time to order and manufacture their equipment before coming on site.

I am sure you must be quite familiar with the requirements of large kitchens, or you could not have sorted out the preliminary schemes so quickly. Although I think I know my job as well as anyone, I must admit to some difficulty in translating what people like you put down on paper as plans. I never seem quite able to put myself up there on the ceiling so I can look down on them. I think it is like languages, you can either learn them or you cannot.

That brings me to the point of this letter. One of those friends of very long acquaintance is Mr. Stover of Bains Marie

Ltd. He will be here for two days next week, the 25th and 26th. When he comes he stays at the Crown at Backburn and what I can only describe as, 'holds court'. He has been doing this for many years now, and he has asked me to invite you along for dinner on the 26th. He will look on this as in the nature of a Royal command. No one ever refuses his invitations, but if you did not wish to come it would of course be understood. If you do come, however, you will meet some people you will be surprised to see there. Unfortunately, I cannot ask you to bring Mrs. Sutton as it is not that kind of an evening, but I will be there.

I am sorry you have not so far been able to accept my standing invitation for a lunchtime drink but now the works are underway there are things I would like to discuss, so do drop in if you can.

Yours sincerely,

The man Stover, who 'holds Court' when he calls at this station on his circuit, is one of that old-fashioned, fast-disappearing brand of businessmen who not only know their job down to the very last detail, but also know the advantage of discussing it in the most congenial surroundings. As Stover's line is kitchen equipment he is up to his eyes in the catering business and prides himself on knowing about food and wine. The Crown has a good but limited cellar and Stover is allowed into it to make his own selection which is, in due course, reverently treated. Mrs. B. is keen for Sooty to go because she knows some of Stover's guests will be at Board-Room level and that there will be some sparkle in the conversation.

There is nothing here even remotely connected with the slightly tawdry commercial traveller approach. To be invited is a privilege with which the placing of an order has nothing whatever to do.

SUTTON TO MRS. BEETON

Dear Mrs. Beeton, 21.8.69

Thank you for your letter regarding, amongst other things, Mr. Stover's invitation to dinner. You make it sound so attractive, how could I possibly refuse? I would be very pleased if you would accept on my behalf, and I shall look forward to meeting you amongst others on the 26th. It sounds as though it should be a very enjoyable evening.

As regards the details of the kitchen, I would like to talk about these with you and Mr. Stover while he is here, as I hope I am right in assuming he is also coming with the object of being available for professional consultation. As you point out, it is time we had all the main decisions taken, and if you had not raised the matter, I would have done so myself by accepting your kind invitation for a lunch-time aperitif. Perhaps you might like to suggest a day next week?

Yours sincerely,

BAINS MARIE & CO. LTD. TO SUTTON

Dear Sir, 28.8.69

Canteen for Rubicon Ltd.

Following the discussion between yourself, our Mr. Stover and Mrs. Beeton of Rubicon, we write to confirm there are some changes to be made to the equipment included in our original quotation. These changes are to bring things into line with the new Catering Act which became law only a few weeks ago. This will mean the substitution of stainless steel worktops in all places where hardwood was proposed and the provision of more hand-washing facilities, among other things. We are sorry to say this will obviously result in an increase in the cost, but this is something beyond our control.

We are preparing a schedule of variations which we will submit for your approval within the coming week. For your information, the administration of this installation will be undertaken by our Mr. Isiah Wells.

Yours faithfully,

This sounds ominous. Stainless steel is a very expensive material although undoubtedly the best for the job. Can it be that Mrs. Beeton will yet succeed in getting a Rolls Royce job?

SUTTON TO BAINS MARIE & CO. LTD.

Dear Sirs, 31.8.69

Rubicon LABWELS

I have today received your revised quotation for the kitchen equipment at the above and am astonished at your temerity in submitting it. Surely the changes brought about by the new

Catering Act cannot result in an increase of almost 25%? No matter what the reason, this new figure cannot be accepted and I would be obliged if you would find some other way of fulfilling the requirements of the Act.

Frankly, I am surprised this situation has arisen at all. New Acts of Parliament do not get on to the Statute Book overnight and surely the provisions of this Bill have been available for scrutiny for a considerable length of time. Secondly, I have looked at the Act myself and find it refers only to 'impervious jointless surfaces' not specifically to stainless steel.

I must therefore request you to look at the job again and to let me have a revised quotation I can advise my clients to accept. There are already a number of extras on this job and it will not stand any more.

Yours faithfully,

This is by no means one of Sooty's best efforts. He is right, of course, in what he says about the Act of Parliament and it is almost certain that Bains Marie & Co. knew what was in the offing when they made their first offer. So, no doubt, did the other tenderers, but none would include the new provisions in case they inflated their figure and lost the job. Mr. Stover's 'gentleman of commerce' image didn't prevent his firm submitting what was really a misleading quotation.

Sutton's indignation, however, is not altogether justified. He should have looked at the Act himself and specified accordingly. One of the most frightening things for a young architect is the vast volume of legislation relating to the building process, and the lack of any index or method of finding out where it is lurking. One can be breaking the law without even being aware of it.

SUTTON TO MRS. BEETON

Dear Mrs. Beeton, 2.9.69

LABWELS

I certainly enjoyed the dinner party hosted by Mr. Stover who seems to have a natural gift for such things. I was particularly pleased to be able to meet on a social level both Mr. Boffin and Mr. Steadman of Rubicon. It helps to find that people are more than just distinguished names within the industrial machine.

Turning now to your kitchen, the problem remains. I am still waiting to hear from Bains Marie with what I hope will be a considerably reduced figure which I can accept without asking my masters' permission. However, I am aware you would like me to accept their revised quotation as it stands, since, quite aside from any Act, it represents the quality you would like to have and simply supports what you know to be the best practice.

There is, however, a further matter which no one has so far mentioned. This is the fact that, as usual, the new Act excludes projects already underway on its coming into operation. As this is defined as the point at which site works are started, there is no compulsion for us to adopt the new standards. To a degree, however, this is beside the point. If, as it would seem, new minimum standards are desirable, they should be maintained, compulsory, or not. The unfortunate thing is that I was not aware of them at the design stage and thus did not allow for them in my estimate of cost. Nor did anyone see fit to enlighten me. I think that what I must now do is to make a clean breast of things to George Turvy, and then leave it to you to exercise your considerable charm to get what you want!

Yours sincerely,

Sutton is advancing in worldly knowledge with long strides. This is the letter of a Machiavelli containing the wisdom of a mind far beyond his tender years. One might be tempted to think he has sought advice, but no, the underlying thread is all his.

SUTTON TO TURVY

Dear George, 2.9.69

LABWELS

I am in a little difficulty over the kitchen equipment. As you know, we had several tenders for this and chose Bains Marie & Co. who are well known to us both. Their tender was just within the PC sum allowed in the Bill.

Unfortunately, there is a new Act covering the standards of equipment in large kitchens, one result of which is to increase the cost. There is no compulsion for us to comply because jobs started before the Act came into operation are excluded, but if these new standards are now considered necessary, it seems to me it would be folly to purposely ignore them. Mrs. Beeton holds this view very strongly and has done so from the outset. Unfortunately, neither she nor Bains Marie thought fit to tell me. I realise I should have been aware of the situation myself, but the truth is that the mass of legislation concerning building is so fast-changing and diffuse that I doubt if there is a person alive who could find it all, let alone understand it.

I have asked Mrs. Beeton to contact you direct and explain her point of view. As I know what this is, I can say here and now that I support it. I know this means another £1,500 on the cost, and that there are other extras, but I do think this is a place where the ship would be spoiled for a ha'porth of tar.

Yours sincerely,

Here again Sutton is at his not inconsiderable best. He accepts part of the blame fairly and squarely, but no one is going to condemn him on the basis of this letter. He is also clearly right in his assessment of the existing situation, and we have noted in the past his ability to present the facts in a way that enables decisions to be made. In military parlance it would be called an 'appreciation' and the ability to make one is as important to an architect as to a soldier (although his life may not depend on it).

TURVY TO SUTTON

Dear Richard, 4.9.69

LABWELS

As usual you have got your way. I have had a visit from Mrs. Beeton (visitation would be nearer the mark). That woman is little short of being a witch and what is more, she knows just about all the important people in this company and is not above using them to gain her ends. She seems to have added you to her string of scalps, so you had better watch your step.

To be fair, she has a genuine passion for her job and a great deal of skill in carrying it out. I have no doubt she is pressing for the right thing to be done. I had a short word with the MD today and despite the extra cost he acquiesced with hardly a murmur. On with the good work!

Yours sincerely,

BAINS MARIE & CO. TO SUTTON

Dear Sir, 4.9.69

Rubicon LABWELS Building

As requested we enclose our revised quotation for the kitchen at the above. As you will see, we have produced a total which is now only 10% above the original, but in our opinion, although it meets the minimum requirements of the new Act, it will not be a good job. If you insist on our doing it this way we have no choice but to comply, but the work will be carried out against our better judgement. The job will not be as good as the one we originally quoted for, because the materials are inferior to the original hardwood in all respects except for the fact that they are impervious.

If the job is done this way we are sure that within a few years there will be maintenance costs arising that will make the extra capital expenditure seem well worthwhile.

We await your further instructions,

Yours faithfully,

PS If you wish, our Mr. Stover is quite prepared to come up for a discussion with your clients.

This is the sort of letter one would expect from a firm like Bains Marie and shows us some of the reasons why they maintain such good customer relations. For them bad workmanship is anathema.

SUTTON TO BAINS MARIE

Dear Sirs, 6.9.69

Rubicon LABWELS

I thank you for your letter received yesterday and appreciate your concern. It is not, however, just a matter of capital and maintenance expenditure. As you know, the taxation of companies often means that high maintenance cost can be off-set against tax, whereas capital expenditure cannot.

Having said this, however, it is my pleasure to inform you that Mrs. Beeton has been instrumental in persuading the management to make a proper job and accept your first revised tender. Commonsense has thus prevailed.

I am instructing the contractors, Knott & Banister to place

their official order with you. In the meantime, you may take this letter as your authority to commence operations.

Yours faithfully,

cc Mrs. Dora Beeton

There is an impishness about this letter which we have not previously observed in Sooty. He keeps them dangling for a little while with his lecture on Capital and Maintenance costs and then gives them the good news.

Dora Beeton will no doubt be pleased to take the credit. It was a good touch to send her a copy.

14

'Bomber' Takes a Dive

SUTTON TO HARRIS

Dear Mr. Harris, 9.9.69

LABWELS Building

I am sorry to have to write in this way so soon after meeting you, but I really cannot tolerate your behaviour at site meetings. I have accepted the most unusual arrangement whereby you chair these meetings, although they are really my meetings, but your behaviour can only be described as barbaric. One of these days I am expecting the whole meeting to walk out in disgust.

I am after all, the architect, and yet you show me no more respect than the least of the sub-contractors. Furthermore, as the leader of the building team, I consider it my duty to see that no one else is being bullied.

I therefore require you to give me your written assurance that you will mend your ways and behave like a reasonable human being, otherwise I shall take steps to have you replaced.

Yours faithfully,

Will he indeed? Has he forgotten that Harris is directly employed by Rubicon? We can divine from this letter that Harris is a real foul-mouthed tyrant, but he must be good at his job or he wouldn't have survived so long.

STEELE (OF K & B) TO SUTTON

Dear Mr. Sutton, 9.9.69

LABWELS

I hope you will excuse me writing to you in this way but I don't know which way to turn. I had a word with Mr. Banister and he said I ought to write to you personally and get it off my chest. The problem is this man Harris. If he goes on the way he is doing, we will never finish the job because there won't be anybody left on the site to do it. One of his favourite little tricks is to walk across still-soft concrete because it hasn't been covered with sand or polythene as specified. Another is take his boot to a section of brickwork if it's not good enough to please him.

If he continues this way I cannot be responsible for him, especially when we get to first scaffold lift. I've seen bricks drop on people before for much less than what Harris is doing. I hope you can please intervene with the employers to see if something can be done for the sake of the job and everyone on it.

Yours faithfully,

It seems nobody loves Harris and it is hardly surprising if he is behaving in this way. Sutton will have to take some sort of action and he has already started the ball rolling by writing to Harris direct.

Men like Harris do crop up occasionally to everyone's discomfort. He probably believes in the practice of condemning everything at first to demonstrate his authority and then easing the pressure a bit later.

HARRIS TO SUTTON

Dear Sir, 11.9.69

Get stuffed, or in other words, up yours.

R. Harris (site engineer)

Brief and to the point, a message that cannot be misunderstood.

SUTTON TO DRAUGHTSMAN

Dear Mr. Draughtsman, 13.9.69

I wonder if you can help me in the matter of your colleague 'Bomber' Harris. He is acting in a thoroughly savage and irresponsible manner, which if it continues will be certain to cause something very unpleasant. I have already written to him direct and I enclose a copy of that letter and his reply, which is right in character. In addition I enclose a letter to me from Steele of K & B. As you can see, he is even more disturbed than I, being in closer contact.

I gather Harris has been with the firm as long as you, or longer, and you must have experienced his activities on jobs of your own. The fact he has survived so long suggests to me he cannot always behave in this way, and I hope you can give me some guidance on how to handle this potentially dangerous situation.

Yours sincerely,

Harris aside, the general tone of this letter suggests that Sutton has achieved what Turvy asked of him in the way of a rapprochement with Draughtsman.

DRAUGHTSMAN TO SUTTON

Dear Mr. Sutton, 15.9.69

I have your letter about Harris and have had a confidential chat with George Turvy and Prop Steadman. We can all appreciate the way you feel, but there is a difficulty. It so happens that during the war Harris served in J.J.s troop as a troop sergeant in the Royal Engineers and they went through some pretty harrowing times together. On one occasion, they got too close to an anti-personnel mine and if it had not been for Harris, it is doubtful if J.J. would have made it back. He has never forgotten this and won't hear a word said against Harris. I think you will understand this.

That said, we accept that you have a problem and things cannot be allowed to go on as they are. Certainly he cannot be permitted to treat you in this disgraceful way. Prop Steadman, who has known him longer than anyone apart from J.J., is going to have a word and we hope this will be effective enough to make the situation tolerable.

You also are right in the idea that Harris gets both feet in at the start to demonstrate he is not going to have any nonsense. Once this is established he eases off a bit. Even he realises that the iron fist can be overdone and counter-productive. We

"If he continues this way I cannot be responsible for him."

suggest you have a quiet word with the builder to encourage him to soldier on until better times are reached.

Yours sincerely,

SUTTON TO BANISTER

Dear Mr. Banister, 16.9.69

I know your agent Mr. Steele consulted you about the problem of 'Bomber' Harris before writing to me. It is a very tricky situation because on taking the matter up with Rubicon, I find that he is a protégé of J. J. Boffin, their Managing Director, with whom he served during the War.

However, it seems our problems are well understood and someone is going to have a try to see if they can be alleviated. In the meantime, we are requested to soldier on and hope for better times. There is one shaft of light, namely that I was right in the surmise that Harris works on the principle of, 'That's for doing nothing, now try something and see what happens' and we can expect him to relax a little before very long. I realize this is not much comfort to you at the moment and that Steele is getting the brunt of it, but it is the best I can do.

Yours sincerely,

STEELE TO SUTTON

Dear Sir, 18.9.69

I have to report an accident which occurred on the site this morning. As Mr. Harris was doing his morning rounds he stepped on a scaffold board, which seemed somehow to have come loose, and fell to the ground. This was only a matter of about six feet but there was a pile of bricks just below and his left leg was broken. I sent for an ambulance and he is in Winterfield General. I reported the matter to Rubicon's safety officer, Mr. Bondsman, who says there will have to be an enquiry, but I had warned Mr. Harris to go carefully, because we hadn't really finished making the scaffolding secure, but all he said was that it had better be or he would have somebodies guts for garters.

Yours faithfully,

It seems that there is after all a merciful providence, but it is likely this one had some help from earthly forces. The broken leg wasn't the whole story either because next we read:

DRAUGHTSMAN TO SUTTON

Dear Mr. Sutton, 19.9.69

LABWELS

I expect the builder has reported to you the accident which occurred on the site yesterday involving our site engineer Mr. R. Harris when he fell from a scaffold and broke his left leg. The hospital has reported it is a double compound fracture and that also due to the fall there is minor damage to the skull, although they do not think this is serious at the moment. It is enough, however, to keep him in there for at least a few weeks. During Mr. Harris's absence his work on site will be carried out by an assistant in his department, Mr. W. Lawson.

The safety and welfare officer, Mr. Bondsman, is to conduct an official enquiry into the incident on behalf of the Company and I expect the Factory Inspector will have something to say. All this is really only the concern of the builder and I don't suppose you need to become involved.

Yours sincerely,

Sighs of relief all round. Steele will probably get his knuckles rapped for running a slack ship, but it will seem worth every bit of it.

15

Higgins Takes the Wheel

SUTTON TO DRAUGHTSMAN

Dear Leslie, 18.9.69

LABWELS and other matters

This has seemed a very long year and I am starting to feel in need of a break. As it's easy to get stale I've decided to get away for a couple of weeks and I've been offered a stretch of the Spey for two weeks' fishing – an offer too good to miss!

While I am away, my chief assistant, Henry Higgins, will be

dealing with all matters which I would normally handle. As he is quite familiar with the job and has, in fact, produced most of the working drawings, he should have no difficulty in dealing with anything which might crop up. As far as I can see there are no immediate problems looming, so it seems to be quite a good time to leave Henry in charge for a couple of weeks.

Yours sincerely,

Sooty shouldn't really tempt providence like this, it's asking for trouble, and of course he gets it.

CORKSCREW BAR CO. TO SUTTON

Dear Sir, 20.9.69

LABWELS Building

We find ourselves in a difficulty in respect of the revised programme for this building. We have a tight schedule to meet and a delay of three weeks, which is outside our control, does affect our capacity to carry out our commitments. We have informed the builders Knott & Banister and they have said they want us on site to suit their *revised* programme, but we cannot just produce capacity out of thin air when we have other commitments. On the other hand, we value our reputation for co-operation whenever it is within our capacity, and we have a suggestion to make.

Our scheme, which you accepted, was based on the use of in-situ concrete, between hollow pots, which needed full formwork, and this is the place where we now have a problem. We do, however, have an alternative system of pre-stressed precast hollow beams which do not require formwork, but still have the advantage of incorporating an in-situ screed as part of the structure. The beams are held in stock suitable for a variety of spans and need only to be cut to length. They virtually eliminate the need for specially bent steel. Using this system we could still meet your programme. We have spoken to Knott & Banister, whom we know quite well, and they would welcome the change.

We await your further instructions.

Yours faithfully,

Poor Higgins. No sooner is Sutton out of the door when he finds himself with a major problem on his hands. Should he say no and stick to the status quo thereby incurring even longer delay than already exists? Should he approve Corkscrew's scheme or just do nothing until Sutton returns in two weeks time? The last alternative must look very attractive, but he is not to be allowed to use it.

DRAUGHTSMAN TO HIGGINS

Dear Sir, 21.9.69

LABWELS Building

I have heard from Knott & Banister that because of delays since they started, the reinforcement fixers cannot move on to site when required and that this will mean an additional delay of three weeks which is very disturbing.

I understand that the Corkscrew Bar Co. have offered an alternative system which they could start at the time they are required because it does not require skilled fixers on site, and that the decision lies in your hands. We are anxious that it is made without further delay.

Yours faithfully,

HIGGINS TO DRAUGHTSMAN

Dear Sir, 21.9.69

When Mr. Sutton left for a two week holiday he was not aware that there was to be a problem over getting the flooring contractors on site when they are needed. I believe you will have been informed of the situation by the builders.

There are three choices open to me:

1. I can accept their suggested alternative system.
2. I can refuse to sanction it.
3. I can advise all parties involved to wait for Mr. Sutton's return, unless, of course, you want to make a decision yourselves.

I am sure Mr. Sutton would be quite willing for this to be done. He should be back in ten days, but that would not be soon enough to alter what will by then have been already put in hand. Unfortunately, he did not leave an address or telephone number where I can contact him.

Yours faithfully,

RECORD OF TELEPHONE MESSAGE

Caller Henry Higgins
To Leslie Draughtsman of Rubicon
Date 22.9.69
Job LABWELS

I discussed the matter of the Corkscrew Bar Co.'s flooring systems with Mr. Draughtsman. I explained that Mr. Sutton is not very enamoured of precast beam floors, but that they have been quite satisfactory if properly fixed and grouted. He was not at all happy at leaving the matter until your return and pointed out that the delays then would be cumulative (two weeks plus three weeks) as the saving of time depends upon an immediate go-ahead being given.

On balance I thought the best course would be to give the go-ahead and so I did.

Henry.

Good for Henry. Faced with a dilemma he has accepted responsibility and firmly taken command. No one is going to blame him even if there are problems later with the floors.

It was very remiss of Sutton not to leave an address and remiss of Higgins or Betzy not to make sure they got one. This is also a flagrant case of buck passing. Rubicon know the score, and could quite well have taken the decision with their highly qualified staff, instead of leaving it to poor old Higgins MSAAT.

HIGGINS TO KNOTT & BANISTER

Dear Sirs, 22.9.69

Rubicon LABWELS

This is to confirm my telephone message that you should instruct the Corkscrew Bar Co. to proceed with their alternative method using precast beams in place of their original proposal.

This is on the understanding that the change means they can adhere to the programme date you require.

Yours faithfully,

The reader should not imagine it is just as simple as it sounds. Any change in the building structure made as late as this inevitably results in a lot of extra work, modifying and reissuing drawings, perhaps to as many as half-a-dozen persons; framing and issuing variation orders and most of all, checking that the alteration does not throw something else completely out of gear. It is certainly not something to be undertaken in haste without due consideration. No doubt Higgins, who seems to be a sensible chap, will have made a careful study of the implications and he had little choice in making his decision.

HIGGINS TO THE CORKSCREW BAR CO.

Dear Sirs, 22.9.69

Rubicon Ltd. LABWELS Building

I confirm that you are authorised to proceed with this work on the basis of your revised scheme using precast beams and structural screed. It is understood there will be no change in the price quotation already approved.

I realise you are not due on the site for a further three weeks, but it is important that I receive your drawings to enable me to consider any side effects before that time. I should really have them in a week's time and I trust you can oblige.

Yours faithfully,

Here is just another example of the extra work which devolves on the architect whenever a change is made, no matter who or what is responsible for it. The real cause of this goes back to the trouble with the foundations, the ramifications of which may well be not yet fully understood.

If a contractor is faced with extra costs not of his own making he is entitled to extra payment. Not so the architect who will only benefit if the changes involve extra cost. Changes which he makes, or has to make, only increase his payment if extra cost results. In this case he is involved in quite a lot of work he should not have had to do, for no return, although the architect himself never looks at it like this. It is a case of professionalism as against commercialism. Both are essential to the well-being of the building industry.

SUTTON TO DRAUGHTSMAN

Dear Leslie, 2.10.69

LABWELS

I am now back from holiday and Higgins has just brought me up to date on the Corkscrew business. I have to accept he was right to make the decision he did, but I must confess that I am not too happy about their precast beam type of construction. Although they are supposed to achieve continuity over the supports it is always a bit dodgy. However, it can be done and the important thing to look out for is the way they insert the continuity bars.

Perhaps you could have a word about this to your clerk of works as I would like him to look carefully at this when they are fixing.

Yours sincerely,

SUTTON TO THE CORKSCREW BAR CO.

Dear Sirs, 2.10.69

Rubicon LABWELS Building

During my absence on two weeks leave, my assistant Higgins made a decision for you to substitute your pre-stressed, precast beam system for the original in-situ concrete scheme, on the grounds that, because of earlier delays on the site, you had to meet a new date. Although this date was later than the original, you were not able to comply because of other commitments. I confirm that he was right to do this.

However, it was also agreed that this would not affect your quotation, and Higgins imagined this was a fair arrangement. You must be aware it is hardly that, because we both know that the use of the precast system effects savings in both time *and* cost. I shall therefore expect a revision of your price in the *downward* direction.

Yours faithfully,

cc. J. le Mesurier

Sutton may be green, but he is not without experience of unit costs, although many would have let this pass. No doubt Corkscrew will concede, but with bad grace.

As the letters pertaining to the middle of the contract period appear to be missing, we take up the narrative again when the structure and enclosure are complete, services are being installed and floors being screeded ready for finishes.

16

The Best-Laid Screeds . . .

MEMO FROM SUTTON TO HIGGINS

12.2.70

These days we always seem to have problems with floor screeds, problems which at one time never cropped up. I suspect it has to do with the speed at which a building dries out when dry forms of construction are used (e.g. precast beams). This time I am taking no chances and have specified a spatter coat using 'Bondtite' on the concrete surfaces and 'Nilshrink' mixed in with the sand and cement of the screed. Both are made by CBP Ltd. It is very important that these products should be used exactly as advised by the maker and I would like you to make it your special responsibility to be on the site when the work starts to see that this does happen

R.J.S.

There are a lot of products of this type on the market. They claim to overcome the twin problems of screeds, poor adhesion and shrinkage, which are interrelated. The principal causes are failing to roughen the surface of the sub floor adequately, laying on a dusty surface, and too much water in the mix. The first two result in loss of adhesion or 'hollowness' and the third in excessive shrinkage and hence cracking and curling at the edges.

Screeders will tend to put too much water in the mix because it makes it easier to work and 'float' off to a smooth finish. Admixtures work by giving good workability with less water in the mix. Another thing that has to be watched is the speed with which the screeds are allowed to dry out. Too rapid drying also leads to shrinkage, so specifications usually insist on the newly-laid screeds being covered with wet sand which has to be rewetted at intervals until the initial drying out period is over. In this age of plastics it is more usual to use polythene sheet for this purpose, but there are doubts as to whether it is just as good (i.e. is it better to maintain dampness, or just restrict evaporation?).

HIGGINS TO KNOTT & BANISTER

Dear Sirs, 13.2.70

LABWELS Building

Mr. Sutton has made me responsible for seeing to it that the screeds are properly laid in accordance with CBP Ltd. instructions for the use of their products, 'Bondtite' and 'Nilshrink'. Would you please advise me of the date you expect to start screeding so that I can arrange for CBP's rep. and myself to be on the site and discuss the procedure. I stress the importance of this meeting, because we have had a lot of troubles with screeds in the past.

Yours faithfully,

Higgins is taking this seriously. No doubt he has had personal experience of screed failures on other jobs (and so have many).

KNOTT & BANISTER TO HIGGINS

Dear Sir, 16.2.70

LABWELS Building

We shall be starting screeding next Monday on the ground floor. Mr. Steele will be there at 9.00 a.m., also our foreman plasterer, 'Billie' Bunter who will be pleased to discuss CBP's instructions with you. We may say that we have never used these items before.

Yours faithfully,

Can one detect a slight note of disapproval or warning in the last sentence? Builders of the K & B type are notoriously suspicious of new products, especially those that have to be added to a mix of any kind.

It is quite normal practice for a foreman plasterer to oversee this kind of work as the trades are related and it is not unusual to refer to screeders as 'good coarse plasterers'.

MEMO FROM HIGGINS TO SUTTON

20.2.70

I met Mr. Steele and Mr. Bunter (foreman plasterer) on the site this morning and I hope I impressed on them the importance of sticking rigidly to the spec. Bunter seems a sensible fellow and I think he got the message. I gather he is not unacquainted with failed screeds himself. Work had started on hacking the concrete with a windy hammer and he says they will wash down before laying any screed. I am to call again in two days time when actual laying should be underway, and I expect CBP's technical rep to be there also.

H.H.

"This is potentially disastrous!"

If anything does go wrong with the screeds it will not be for want of trying on the part of Sutton and Higgins.

SUTTON TO KNOTT & BANISTER

Dear Sirs, 27.2.70

LABWELS

When I called on the site this morning I was horrified to see that after all the emphasis placed on avoiding rapid drying of the screeds, your men were actually using calor gas dryers in areas where screeds were not even covered. This is potentially disastrous and I gave immediate instructions that the practice must cease and the screeded areas covered immediately.

I must ask you for an explanation of this strange behaviour.

Yours faithfully,

KNOTT & BANISTER TO SUTTON

Dear Sir, 1.3.70

We have your letter re the screeds and hasten to tender our apologies. We assure you that what happened did not arise from any lack of understanding of your instructions as we ourselves have had our problems with screeds, which we used not to have years ago. As you know, we also have plasterers at work and there is a need for them to make good progress if we are to keep to our agreed programme. They are working with gypsum which is an altogether different story to compo.* We have to try and allow painters in, in less than a month and hence the dryers.

Fortunately not a lot of damage can have been done because there were only two places where screed and plaster were green at the same time. We have of course corrected the situation and will keep an eye on the areas in question.

Yours faithfully,

It sometimes seems there is no way to ensure things turn out the way intended. Sutton has bent over backwards to avoid problems with the screeds only to have some over-enthusiastic plasterers turning on calor-gas heaters all over the place, with screeds still not dried. He will do well to check and record the 'two places only' which Knott & Banister say were affected. One would not expect Knott & Banister to try and wriggle out of anything which was their fault, but in these situations, where more than one trade is involved, the complexities would confound Solomon himself.

**Cement and Sand 1:3*

KNOTT & BANISTER TO SUTTON

Dear Sir, 7.3.70

LABWELS

The Blackpool Rock Asphalt Co., who are to lay the ground-floor asphalt sub-floor, are due to start next week according to the programme. They have been on site and tested the screeds with a moisture meter and are not satisfied that they are yet dry enough for them to start. They would agree to start if you gave your approval and we would be pleased to see you on the site to discuss this situation.

Yours faithfully,

Sutton would be an idiot to fall for this one. Such a risk could only be taken if the maintenance of the programme were absolutely vital, and with the possible consequences fully realised. Such decisions do sometimes have to be taken.

NOTES ON A SITE MEETING HELD TO DISCUSS THE CONDITION OF THE GROUND-FLOOR SCREEDS BEFORE COMMENCING ASPHALT WORK

Date: 10.3.70
Present: A. Steele (Knott & Banister)
L. Draughtsman (Rubicon)
R. Harris (Rubicon)
B. Bunter (Browning & Skim, Plasterers)
S. Limmer (Blackpool Rock Asphalt Co.)
R. J. Sutton (Architects)
H. Higgins (Architects)

An inspection of the screeds was made and Mr. Limmer produced a moisture meter and tested in a number of places. In general he thought there was about 10% too much water present for absolute safety, but there were a couple of places which were already dry enough. Not surprisingly, these turned out to be the areas where the plasterers had been using calor-gas heaters to accelerate the drying of the plaster.

A visual inspection was also made and confirmed the meter

readings i.e. those areas appeared lighter in colour than the others. None of the screeds felt damp to the touch.

Mr. Limmer estimated that unless dryers were now brought in, at least another week, perhaps more, would be needed before his men could safely start. He saw no reason why dryers should not be used now the initial drying stage was over, but he would give no guarantees other than for his own work.

Mr. Draughtsman and Mr. Harris were both concerned about the delay which would also put back the date for the flooring sub-contractors to start. Mr. Harris expressed himself in his usual forceful way. Mr. Limmer, who was meeting Mr. Harris for the first time seemed somewhat taken aback, but still declined to be bullied into both sticking to the programme and, guaranteeing his work, which was what Harris was after.

Mr. Bunter thought that with the benefit of his long years of experience the screeds seemed about ready. Mr. Steele of Knott & Banister thought the same, but no one was prepared to take the risk and accept the consequences of starting asphalting straight away, not even Harris. A good deal of tapping was done but no definite hollowness was found. In the end, it was left to the architects to make a decision, which was inevitably to start now on the two dry areas and review the position after a week. B.R.A.C. accepted this without complaint.

R.J.S.

In spite of having put Higgins on to this one, Sutton clearly thinks it important enough to bring in the top brass. Everyone seems to have been moving with extreme caution and the final word was left to Sutton but 'doubtless, he hasn't heard the last of it.

17

A Question of Style

BOFFIN TO SUTTON

Dear Mr. Sutton, 16.2.70

LABWELS Building

Our chairman, Sir Isaac Gildenstein, always takes an interest in any buildings being constructed for the company, particularly when, as in this case, he expects to be using at least some part of them when he visits us. This time his particular interest is in the Chairman's Dining Room.

Sir Isaac would like to discuss this with you in the near future and for that purpose would like to see you in London, where he can take you to other dining rooms and board rooms in the City to indicate the sort of thing he has in mind at Winterfield. His wife trained as an interior designer, and he usually likes her to have some say in the matter.

I have given him your address and you may expect to hear from him shortly.

Yours sincerely,

This is enough to terrify any young architect and we can only hope that Sooty will conduct himself bravely when he enters the lion's den. The Royal command came a few days later. The letter is typed on an electric machine with a carbon ribbon and proportional spacing. The heading is embossed in restrained characters and from an address in Threadneadle Street. There is nothing so vulgar as the mention of a Limited company.

GILDENSTEIN TO SUTTON

Dear Mr. Sutton, 18.2.70

Although I have not so far had the pleasure of meeting you, I hear encouraging reports of the work you are doing for one of my companies at Winterfield. As the new building seems quite well advanced, I feel this might be an appropriate moment to discuss the interior of the Chairman's dining room.

I must state it plainly from the beginning that I am very fastidious about the interior finishing of such rooms and that I consider it important they convey a traditional sense of efficiency, solidity of purpose and impeccable good taste. I therefore always prefer to settle such details with the architect myself. In this I am fortunate to have the help of a wife who was trained in interior design and I rely greatly on her advice.

To give you some idea of the way I like things done, perhaps you might care to call on me in London and I will personally conduct you round some of my board rooms and dining rooms in the City. Wednesday, a week hence, would suit me very well at 2.00 pm, and I would be grateful if you could confirm acceptance of these arrangements by telephoning my secretary, Mrs. Hyde, at the above number.

Yours sincerely,

SUTTON TO GILDENSTEIN

Dear Sir Isaac, 19.2.70

Thank you for your letter. This is to confirm my telephone arrangement with Mrs. Hyde that I shall be pleased to see you at your home at 2.00 pm this Wednesday coming and will hold myself at your disposal for the remainder of that day.

Yours sincerely,

A bit curt perhaps, but on reflection I think not. Sutton is to meet a man whose standing is right out of his league, but it would be a great mistake to crawl. He is a member of an honourable profession, and hence his equal in status at least. Gildenstein will expect no more, no less.

SUTTON TO MCDONALD

Dear Ian, 25.2.70

In the past you have been good enough to advise me on problems where your experience has far exceeded mine. I don't want to trespass unduly on your time so I will be as brief as possible. I fancy that you may have faced this same situation except of course that in your case your client was also your employer.

The Labwels building contains a chairman's dining room, and so I was summonsed to the great man's home in Albany to take instruction and be shown examples of other rooms in the City where he has been in control. His name is Sir Isaac Gildenstein and he is blessed with a wife who trained in interior design (a failed architect I fancy).

We went first to his office which is knee deep in pile and panelled in mahogany (solid, not veneered). In the centre is a kingsized mahogany desk with tooled leather gilded top bearing a leather bound blotter, silver inkstand and three pens, nothing more. Tea is brought in on a silver tray. The china is Dresden. I think you may get the general idea.

Our tour of inspection (by Rolls) took in three boardrooms and one dining room, which apart from size were virtually identical, clearly the work of one person. On enquiring who

"The tour of inspection took in three boardrooms . . ."

was responsible I was told "Strumpets", who as you will know are about the best known firm in the trad. interior business. I was told also that they will be doing this one, there is to be no competition. Lady G. will also assist.

The principal furniture requirement is a table to seat 15 and 15 chairs, all Chippendale, original if they can be found, repro if not. The walls are to be panelled in mahogany (solid of course), with raised panels and bolection moulds. There is to be an Adam style ceiling, crystal chandeliers and Adam fireplace. (How those chaps did get about.)

I hardly dared ask, but if the room is to be yet another replica of those it will have to have Georgian divided windows, and how am I supposed to reconcile those with the rest of the building?

What am I now to do? I feel that it is my duty to try and get this changed and must have at least one go at him. Perhaps the MD might have some views; after all he is the chief executive (but Gildenstein controls the money). What do you think?

Yours,

Chairman and Directors have a habit of laying down the law to architects, whether they be engaged on a commission or directly employed in their own company. They are also firmly of the opinion that anything modern in either buildings or furniture is bound to be in tinny bad taste, and they feel much safer with objects at least a hundred years old. Such captains of industry are also frequently influenced by their wives in such matters (who have usually exhausted the scope for interior decoration at home).

SUTTON TO TURVY (STRICTLY CONFIDENTIAL)

Dear George, 27.2.70

I am sorry to have to come to you with a rather delicate problem, but it is a matter of some concern. Unfortunately, I think it is my duty to consult you before accepting the instructions I have had from Sir Isaac for the Chairman's Dining Room in the proposed LABWELLS building. These are to the effect that I have to closely liaise with the firm Strumpets, and Lady Gildenstein to produce a fake Georgian interior with mahogany panelling, Adam ceiling, 'shell niches' and Chippendale furniture (real if I can find it).

I am very unhappy about this because the whole thing strikes a completely false note in an otherwise contemporary building. I don't make any great claim that the new building is a masterpiece, but I do think it is turning out quite well and that it will one day be an asset to your works. The worst feature of these proposals is the instruction I have received to use Georgian sash windows which of course will look utterly ridiculous from the outside. Sir Isaac seems oblivious to this. I expect you will have some views, and if you think fit, you might also have a word with Mr. Boffin about it.

Yours sincerely,

TURVY TO SUTTON (STRICTLY CONFIDENTIAL)

Dear Richard, 2.3.70

I think you are treading on dangerous ground. None of us knows our Chairman very well and I'm afraid most Chairman are like that; they live in a very remote and rarified atmosphere. We do have a common language, but it has only a very limited vocabulary. We do the work, they provide the money, and they like us to be constantly reminded of this. The lack of control on spending for the purposes in which you are now involved, is typical of this approach to business. Managing Directors are not in the same category at all, and Works Managers even less so. I have no doubt that both J.J. and even Harry Steadman are with you all the way, but they are not going to say so.

I am sorry, Sooty, but I think you are just going to have to grit your teeth and get on with those g. windows. I know you can concede gracefully from past experience, and I am sure you would not want to be struck off our list of architects (which at the moment includes only you). I also feel sure, that with your usual skill at resolving apparently irreconcilable problems, some unlooked for solution may gradually present itself.

I have already had words with J.J. and Harry Steadman and whilst they are both sympathetic, they are not going to stick their necks out and risk the Chairman's displeasure over what seems to them a matter of comparative triviality. If they were more concerned I would go along with them, but as they feel it is purely a matter of personal taste I too must refrain. I'm sorry, but there it is. I shall be very interested, however, to hear

how you propose to deal with the situation.
Yours sincerely,

This is the frankest and perhaps the friendliest letter so far from Turvy to Sutton, and Sutton should learn a valuable lesson i.e. not to go around all the time with his conscience hanging out. Turvy as the older man, is asking him to show a little more realism and accept there are some orders that cannot be questioned. As we know from previous experience, however, Sutton can, at times be extremely stubborn. He decides to go it alone.

SUTTON TO GILDENSTEIN

Dear Sir Isaac, 4.3.70
Rubicon Ltd. LABWELS Building

Since our recent meeting I have been giving much thought to certain stylistic problems arising from your proposals for the Chairman's Dining Room in this building. To be completely frank, I am writing because I sincerely feel the design treatment you and Lady Gildenstein clearly favour places me in a difficult professional position. In short, my conscience as an architect is t roubled.

I feel you may not be sufficiently aware that architects of my generation are constantly striving to follow the traditions of our predecessors in trying to create buildings which are as truly representative of this century as were the great Gothic cathedrals of theirs. It is true we have not yet found a totally satisfying vocabulary capable of resolving all the problems arising from the increasingly complex services and wide range of usages we are required to cater for. However, these problems will not be solved by simply reverting to the manners of a bygone age, however elegant these were. If the Georgians themselves could have made large sheets of glass, they would have used them.

I hope you will not think I am trying to lecture you on architecture through the ages. I felt I must simply explain why I am reluctant to treat these rooms in the way you suggest. It would be an anachronism. I do find it difficult to understand how you as chairman of a company at the forefront of industrial progress in its field, should wish to go back two centuries for the interior design of rooms to be used by its top management. I notice that on my visit to you and Lady Gildenstein, I was not carried round the City of London in a sedan chair. Furthermore, if we are really going to follow our predecessors properly, you should have candles as the sole means of illumination and a coal-burning fireplace.

My object in saying all this is to ask you to at least consider an alternative on which I was already working when you sent for me. I do assure you there is no need for a contemporary interior design to be brash or gaudy. At the same time, I shall start a scheme on the lines you have suggested and, of course, the final decision is yours.

Yours sincerely,

'Instructed' would have been a better word than 'suggested'. Sutton is here going as far as he dare, and possibly a little further.

GILDENSTEIN TO SUTTON

Dear Mr. Sutton, 8.3.70

LABWELS Dining Room

Thank you for your letter concerning your theories of architectural progress. The point you make about designing these rooms in the vernacular of a bygone age is, in fact, right at the heart of my preferences. It is precisely because of the almost intolerable strains and tensions of modern industrial society, that I believe important decisions should be made in the atmosphere of a more leisurely and elegant age.

I am sorry, Mr. Sutton, if I appear curt, but being a busy man I have no further time to pursue this matter. Please carry out my instructions. If you have any difficulty in remembering your artistic voabulary, I'm sure you will find both Strumpets and Lady Gildenstein to be of invaluable assistance. I will expect to see your scheme shortly.

Yours sincerely,

And that, it seems, is that! No room for misunderstanding there. Sutton will just have to make the best of it. In the matter of outdated solutions to modern problems Sir Isaac has neatly turned the tables on Sooty and it is probably not the first time he has used this ploy.

However, in the end all turns out well – see letter from Turvy to Sutton dated 6.6.70 (page 132). Sutton must have a guardian angel.

18

Rights of Light

TURVY TO SUTTON

Dear Sooty, 1.3.70

LABWELS

You may remember that when we were considering the early schemes for this building the point arose that due to the restricted site we would be building right up to our boundary and would have windows overlooking our neighbour's land. These people (WACC Ltd.) manufacture wire and cable, and form an offshoot of Leverpullers with whom we have always had good relations. You may recollect that although at the time I was going to speak to them about it, I was so sure there would be no objection that I didn't bother.

I have now had a call from WACC Ltd. and they pointed out that if our new windows are not obstructed, a right of light will be eventually acquired over their land. While they have no immediate plans for building on this land, they may need to do so in the future and naturally they do not want part of their land sterilised by a right acquired by the adjoining property.

This is all quite understandable but the thing is, how can it be best arranged? I have no previous experience of rights of light and everyone seems to have different ideas as to how they are acquired and how extensive they are. As architects are usually thought to be knowledgable about such rights, I wondered if you would care to give me your views on the situation?

Yours,

The question of rights of light has caused a great deal of heart-searching for many a long year. As Turvy says, architects are supposed to know something about it, but, as with many other points of law, there are no actual regulations, only case history.

SUTTON TO TURVY

Dear George, 7.3.70

LABWELS Rights of Light

This is to put on paper the main points of our telephone discussion about rights of light. As I said, there is no statute law on this vexed question, and hence no hard and fast rules which can be applied to every situation. To the best of my knowledge, whenever a dispute has arisen, the settlement has been based on the maintenance of 'adequate' daylighting. The decision as to what is 'adequate' has to take into account all relevant circumstances, including the purpose for which the light is needed. Some purposes of course need more light than others.

There is a rule of thumb (and that is all it is) that nothing should encroach above a line drawn at 45° from the cill of the window in question. This, of course, takes no account of the situation in the horizontal plane and a window close to the end of an obstruction, whatever it is, will obviously get more light than one somewhere near the middle. Still, lots of agreements have been reached on the good old 45° rule and have been found satisfactory.

None of this has any connection with Part K of the Building Regulations which controls the provision of open space outside windows to maintain adequate ventilation. This space has to be within the boundary of the site.

One way for WACC Ltd. to preserve their rights would be to erect hoardings in front of your windows at suitable intervals of time. Here again there seems to be no one opinion as to how long such periods should be. It is generally reckoned that it takes 20 years to acquire a right of light or right of way, but footpaths which are open to the public as a privilege, are usually closed for one day per year to prevent a right of way being conceded.

One point to be noted here is that the building which existed on the site when we started, and which has been incorporated, has windows on the boundary and these have already acquired a right of light. I can't quite see how this helps us at the moment, but it may come in handy in any discussions with WACC which may follow.

I had a case recently which went to council's opinion on both sides, but I hope we don't get as far as that. Since there seems to be goodwill on both sides I would have thought a simple agreement drawn up by your (or their) solicitors stating that you renounce the acquisition of rights for these windows would meet the case.

Yours,

Sooty's discourse on the vexed question of rights of light is really quite masterly. As he says, there is no single or simple answer to any individual case – frequently a matter of considerable annoyance to people faced with the problem.

A really well-fought right of light case can be fascinating. I have personal knowledge of a case where a complainant acknowledged a right of light, but contested there was no 'RIGHT OF VIEW'. This was based on the fact that the existing windows, before alteration, had been glazed with obscure glass and were now to have clear glass. The matter went to council's opinion which finished, after several pages, with the recommendation to consult a 'good architect'. There is not, and never has been, a 'right of view', but it just goes to show how far the law will go to establish a principle, and how little it counts.

TURVY TO SUTTON

Dear Sooty, 9.3.70

LABWELS

Many thanks for your limpid explanation of the complications of the law regarding rights of light. We must count ourselves lucky to have you on our side.

I should explain that there appears to have been a change in the management structure of WACC and that the friendly arrangement which I originally assumed to exist has unfortunately changed. It seems our relationship is to be based on strict commercial principles in future and although some would say this is inevitable, I must confess to a preference for the less formal relationships of old.

I enclose a copy of the rather chilling letter I have received from the new Managing Director of WACC Ltd. and would be grateful for your opinion as to what sort of reply I should make.

Yours sincerely,

JAMES STRUTT TO TURVY (COPY)

Dear Sir, 7·3·70

I am informed you are the person to contact as regards the new building now almost completed adjoining our western boundary. I notice it has windows on both floors directly overlooking our site. This letter is to inform you such a state of affairs is not acceptable.

Quite naturally I had assumed you would have obtained permission for this from my predecessor, but my enquiries have yielded no such record of this if, indeed, it ever existed. In my view, to just go ahead and build to this plan without even informing us of your intentions seems not only unprofessional but very discourteous. I would be pleased to have your comments, together with your proposals to rectify the situation.

Yours faithfully,

SUTTON TO TURVY

Dear George, 10.3.70

LABWELS

Many thanks for your letter and the enclosed copy letter from WACC's new MD. He sounds a bit of a tartar. If possible I think we should avoid getting involved with solicitors over this and try the friendly approach first. After all, we are not doing any damage to their site and you have always been good neighbours.

Yours sincerely,

TURVY TO STRUTT (COPY)

Dear Sir, 13·3·70

Thank you for your letter on the subject of our new laboratory and welfare building. I must immediately apologise for not having informed you of our intentions. This was purely an oversight and I can assure you, no discourtesy was intended. I hope we can settle the matter amicably.

What you can now see is the full extent of our intentions. There will never be any more openings in that wall. The windows are not large and have only small opening lights for ventilation. The rooms will only be in use at lunchtime and shift change times. I think you will agree they cannot cause any inconvenience or damage to your site. I realise that you probably have in mind the question of rights of light. If so, we would be prepared to enter into an agreement whereby we renounce any rights we might in time acquire over your land. If you wish I could have a draft document drawn up to that effect.

I look forward to receiving your comments.

Yours faithfully,

STRUTT TO TURVY (COPY)

Dear Sir, 15.3.70

Rights of Light

I have received your letter about this matter and it does not bring me any comfort. In putting windows on our boundary you are taking an unpardonable liberty and the situation is not to be tolerated. Who is to say that in twenty years time we might not wish to erect a new building on our boundary and find ourselves baulked by your rights of light?

I am not at all happy about an agreement which is only on paper and I fear I must insist on something more concrete. These openings must be bricked up, or sealed with something equally solid.

Yours faithfully,

This is stupid. If paper agreements are not acceptable how does he run his business. Strutt must also know something about rights of light because this is the first mention of twenty years. He has, however, no authority to insist that the openings be closed by Rubicon, only to take some action on his site to block the light which the windows enjoy.

It is possible that he can get at them on another count. Since 1965 there have been rules in the Building Regulations about the area of openings in external walls and very little is permitted in walls on or near to a boundary. Is it possible that something as obvious as this could get past the eagle eye of Hardnut, the Winterfield Borough Council building inspector? It seems it has.

STRUTT TO TURVY (COPY)

Dear Sir, 17.3.70

Following the writing of my last letter it occurred to me there must be reasons in addition to the question of rights of light, which make it undesirable to have windows actually on a boundary. The problem of fire would be one such instance.

Accordingly, I have spoken to our own architect who assures me there are regulations about this, and that your building does not comply. I must therefore again request you to block up these openings. If this is not done, I shall have no alternative but to report the matter to Winterfield Council.

Yours faithfully,

A very awkward situation for Rubicon. What, if any, action Winterfield Council would take if the matter were reported we can only speculate on as I doubt if there is any case history of such a situation. By rights, what the Council should do in such an event is to inform Rubicon that they must rectify the situation. However, as this would amount to a confession of its own guilt in not enforcing the regulations properly, Rubicon could well come back to the Council for compensation amounting to the additional cost involved. In any case the report would presumably go to Hardnut who would no doubt sweep it promptly under the carpet (unless he could find a way to put the blame on someone else). In the event it does not come to this.

SUTTON TO TURVY

Dear George, 20.3.70

LABWELS

Thank you for the copies of the latest letters from your new neighbour Strutt. He certainly seems to have a vindictive streak in his character.

You have been kind enough not to comment on my part in the slip-up with regard to the Building Regulations, but obviously I have to share the blame for this with the Council. The fact is that this part of the Regulations has only been in force since 1965 and until now I have not had occasion to refer to it as I have not previously had a building hard up by or very close to a boundary. I realise this is not your concern, but none of us is perfect and I can only crave your indulgence.

We must now try to establish the best course of action in the circumstances and I am turning over an idea which might well solve both problems at once. With the windows as they now stand there should be a space of 1½ metres minimum from wall to boundary. Why not offer to buy a strip of land 1½ metres wide from WACC? This then puts you right with the Building Regulations and would go a long way towards solving your rights of light situation. Even if WACC did decide to build right up to their new boundary you would still have some light from these windows, and what is more important, natural ventilation.

I have no doubt Strutt's instincts will be to turn down any such offer, but I suspect he is a mercenary man, and for such people everything has its price. This you would have to weigh against the inconvenience of having your light blocked out. I say inconvenience advisedly, because it is really no more than that. On the first floor most of the lighting comes from roof lights and on the ground floor the rooms are only occupied for about one hour a day and artificial lighting is not all that objectionable. There is sufficient spare capacity in the main extract fan to boost the air change rate to the necessary degree. Should you ever decide to add the third storey you would lose your roof lights but this could be dealt with at the time). There is therefore no need for us to go cap in hand to the aggressive Mr. Strutt.

There is also another interesting and, so far as I am aware, undocumented possibility. There is, I believe no such thing as a 'right of air,' but there is nothing prohibiting a building from drawing its ventilation air from over an adjoining owner's land. If for example, a building on a boundary has ventilation openings in that side I wonder whether the adjoining owner could seal these off by building right up to them and if so, would the first owner have any redress?

The regulations referred to are contained in Part E and are intended to prevent the spread of fire. It is interesting to note that by simply redrawing the boundary the building can be made to comply, although there is absolutely no change at all to the situation on site.

Sutton seems to be taking the whole matter rather light heartedly. He perhaps does not realise that Rubicon may see his culpability in a more serious light.

TURVY TO SUTTON

Dear Richard, 22.3.70

LABWELS

Thank you for your letter and the suggestion it contained.

The further we go into this matter the more complex it seems to become. I am writing to Strutt to make the offer you suggest and will let you know the outcome. A copy of my letter is enclosed.

Yours sincerely,

This seems a little curt for Turvy. Is Sutton's levity starting to bug him?

TURVY TO STRUTT (COPY)

Dear Mr. Strutt, 22.3.70

Rights of light etc.

Since receiving your two letters I have spoken to R. J. Sutton, our architect for this project, and he confirms there was an oversight on both his part and that of the Borough Engineer. Consequently, the situation is as you describe. Mr. Sutton also advises us that the purchase of $1\frac{1}{2}$ metres of land in a strip along the present boundary would resolve the matter, being the required distance from the boundary for the extent of the openings in that side of the building. Such a purchase would also alleviate the right of light situation and we would still be prepared to indemnify you against the acquisition of a right of light at any time in the future.

We think this suggestion has a lot of merit and would like you to consider it seriously. If you also approve, perhaps you would be kind enough to inform us of the value you put on the land in question.

Yours sincerely,

STRUTT TO TURVY (COPY)

Dear Mr. Turvy, 27.3.70

Thank you for your letter concerning the possible purchase of a strip of land on our mutual boundary. I am sure you must appreciate that such a sale has very little to recommend it other than an extremely attractive price. This being the case, I leave it to you to make us an offer.

Yours sincerely,

TURVY TO STRUTT (COPY)

Dear Sir, 30.3.70

Rights of light etc.

Thank you for your letter of the 27th. We would have preferred you to state your price, but since you have invited us to make an offer, I would suggest something in the region of £500. The actual land area is about 100 m^2 and it can surely not be worth more than £5 per m^2.

I await your decision.

Yours sincerely,

STRUTT TO TURVY (COPY)

Dear Mr. Turvy, 2.4.70

Thank you for your letter of the 30th March. I am sorry to say the offer contained in it can only be regarded by my company as derisory and I must ask you to think again. A price of £5 per m^2 might be the general value of land in this area but we are not in the business of selling land. As I have already said, we have no incentive whatever for making this sale other than to oblige you, and you must expect to pay for the privilege. I suggest £2,000 might be nearer the mark and that is my final word on the matter.

Yours sincerely,

TURVY TO STRUTT (COPY)

Dear Mr. Strutt, 4.4.70

Thank you for your letter. We accept your offer and I am instructing our solicitors to get in touch with you to arrange the conveyancing. I take it that once this purchase is completed the question of rights of light will be settled.

Yours sincerely,

Turvy would no doubt discuss this unhappy matter with Boffin before agreeing to pay. It won't make either of them happy, but they must have thought it worthwhile to have peace of mind and not to be left with a problem which might have gone smouldering on for some considerable time.

Sutton's popularity is going to suffer since in the end it was his slip-up with the Building Regulations which determined the outcome, rather that Turvy's failure to take up the question of rights of light with WACC.

TURVY TO SUTTON

Dear Richard, 4.4.70

LABWELS

To bring you up to date I am enclosing copies of my latest correspondence with Strutt. As you see we have settled the matter, but at a cost which could only have been demanded of someone trapped in a corner.

In reaching this decision I have had to discuss it with J.J. and now that he is fully in the picture, I am sorry to say he will be looking to you to make at least some contribution. I have his instructions to put this to you and obtain your comment.

Yours sincerely,

This the tough commercial approach which doesn't really suit Turvy. However when a question of negligence arises, bleak commerce usually rears it's ugly head.

In the past the attitude of a patron to his architect was of a more paternal nature. The Duke of Marlbrough would not have expected Vanbrugh to pay for any mistakes he might have made whilst building Blenheim. The master takes full responsibility for the actions of his servant and that was the ethic controlling their relationship. Until recently, this was still the case, not perhaps in law, but in practice. Within the last two or three decades the attitude has changed and both client and builder may at times put the architect between Scylla and Charybdis. There have been quite a number of actions in court in which the architect has been heavily involved and this is sad because both client and builder may well be large organisations with substantial sums at their disposal. The architect, on the other hand, is seldom in the same financial league and has to rely on professional indemnity insurance to defend him. Such insurance is getting both harder to get and more costly, to the extent that not all architects can afford it (especially those who most need it). In this case, only a small amount is involved and one would have thought Rubicon could pay up and look pleasant. After all, they are getting a piece of land in return.

SUTTON TO TURVY

Dear George, 6.4.70

LABWELS

Thank you for your letter. I am so pleased to see you have settled the matter with Strutt. As I expected, he had his price.

I am sorry to learn you feel aggrieved over my part in the unfortunate matter, but I should say I have not attempted to conceal anything and also that I immediately accepted the blame for the Building Regs contravention. However, had the question of rights of light not cropped up, the rest of the story would never have been known, and your building would have been perfectly satisfactory. The position of the boundary in this particular instance was really quite irrelevant.

As you may be aware, architects do not have vast capital reserves to fall back on, and what may be a trifle to you is quite a lot to me. I am afraid the sum of £2,000 comes into that category.

Another point of relevance is this. You may remember that at the start of the affair I informed you that even if WACC did seal off your windows, the building could still function quite satisfactorily, and that it was not technically essential to settle with WACC at all. The decision to settle was yours and in the circumstances I do not think I should be asked to contribute at all. Such a suggestion also cuts across the proper relationship between client and architect – that of patron and artist, which I thought existed in our case.

Yours sincerely,

This seems fair. Although Sutton did not directly mention it, it was really Turvy's omission to consult WACC over the right of light business which was the root cause of the entire affair. Turvy doesn't seem to have replied to this letter so we must take it that the matter was discussed over the phone, or during a visit. The likelihood is that Sutton was let off the hook, but his popularity with the client has obviously suffered, as we see in the next batch of letters.

19

More about Fees

SUTTON TO TURVY

Dear George, 3.5.70

LABWELS – Fees

You may recall that when I presented my first fee account I

mentioned that fees on alteration work were based on a higher percentage of the cost than for new work. This is because, generally speaking, there is more work for the architect, in relation to the cost of the job, in alteration work and the normal scale for new work would usually result in a loss rather than a profit for the architect. You might appreciate this more when I tell you that on a small alteration job I did two years ago the cost to me was nearly four times the fee received.*

In your case, only a comparatively small part of the job is alteration work. However, we are now far enough through for the quantity surveyors to make a close estimate of the value of that work, and they have given me a figure of £7,750. The scale for new work of this amount would be 8.5% but for work to existing buildings the scale is 12.5%. You can check this in the copy of the RIBA Conditions of Engagement which I sent you earlier.

There will be, therefore, an extra fee of 4% on the value of the work to the existing building, amounting at the final stage to £310. The enclosed account is based on completion of all the design and production drawing stages plus 50% of the site construction stage. I am sure you will agree that this stage has been passed. It amounts to 87½% of the total fee, or as close as we can estimate it before the final account is settled.

Yours,

All very true, but is doubtful if Turvy will like it. Whenever the subject of fees of any kind is raised, whether by doctors, lawyers, estate agents or architects, there lurks a suspicion in the client's mind that he is being taken for a ride. This is especially true when, as in this case, something extra appears towards the end of the job. The additional sum of £310 is not very much but it will rankle.

Perhaps it would have been best to forget the whole thing for the sake of a paltry £310 but the Conditions of Engagement do not allow of this. They state quite clearly that the scale is a minimum and architects are obliged to treat it as such. To charge less is a breach of the professional ethic, known as undercutting, the intention being to see to it that they get their work on grounds of merit, not price. Charging more than the scale is all right, but hardly ever happens for obvious reasons. The question

**In saying this Sutton is including his own time at some appropriate value.*

often arises 'how is a young architect to get work by reason of merit when he has nothing to show'? There is no answer to that.

TURVY TO SUTTON

Dear Richard, 10.5.70

LABWELS – Fees

I have your latest interim account for fees and whilst I have no comment on the stage reached, I am a bit surprised and disappointed by the extra on the work to the existing building. When we started off I was under the impression that your fee was a simple matter of 6% of the cost of the work. Now this seems not to be so and we are having to pay extra.

As far as I can remember, we have not had to pay any extra to the architects we have used previously and I doubt whether J.J. will take too kindly to it. I do hope you are not going to spring any more surprises of this nature on us.

Yours,

The delay in replying to Sutton's letter in itself suggests that Turvy didn't like it and is going to make Sutton sorry he has committed an indiscretion. What is more, Sutton will doubtless be made to wait for payment. Turvy has conveniently forgotten that when he received Sutton's first fee account he was warned there would be something extra for alteration work and out-of-pocket expenses. He now seems to be saying that he doesn't want to know about these either.

No one likes the sordid subject of money, but it has to be faced sometime or other and the sooner the better. Much the best way is to include everything that is going to become due eventually in the first interim account. Costs that are not known, such as expenses, can be estimated and an appropriate portion included. In this way it may even be possible to give something back at the end of the day, which is always a welcome move. The Conditions of Engagement state that all the architect's expenses incurred in the execution of the project are recoverable and include, all printing and copying costs, hotel and travelling expenses, plus all other disbursements. Telephone and postal charges can only be claimed by prior written agreement with the client.

SUTTON TO TURVY

Dear George, 12.5.70

I am sorry that my claim for extra fees for alteration work

has caused you concern. I am surprised to learn these have not cropped up in the course of work with other architects and I must assume these previous occasions have only involved new work. If not, then those architects were breaking their Code of Conduct, which clearly states these charges *must* be made. Not to do so is a form of price undercutting which can work to the detriment of their colleagues, as in a sense they are seeking to obtain work by lowering their charges. To be strictly correct, I should ask you for their names and report them to the Royal Institute. However, I do not propose to do so.

In my own defence, I should say that I gave you fair warning this question would arise. If you refer back to my letter of 15.5.69 you will see that I mention both alteration work and expenses. I'm afraid that the question of expenses will have to be faced at final account stage.

Yours sincerely,

TURVY TO SUTTON

Dear Richard, 15.3.70

I almost get the feeling you are deliberately trying to provoke me on this matter of fees. You seem to think that any amount less than a couple of thousand pounds is of no importance to Rubicon just because we are big. Once again costs are rising, although it is barely a month since we set down £2,000 for a strip of land we could just as well have done without. What can I say to disabuse you of the notion our purse is bottomless? As regards your expenses I would be grateful if you could inform Draughtsman how much you expect these to amount to as I shall shortly be leaving on a business trip to Tokyo.

Yours sincerely,

It seems clear there are stormy waters ahead for Sutton as and when he claims his expenses. This shouldn't be so. Employers should not try to push their architects into breaking their own Code of Practice, which has as its primary purpose, the protection of the employer's interests, by making ability the only criterion for selection.

SUTTON TO TURVY (STRICTLY CONFIDENTIAL)

Dear George, 17.5.70

I am sorry that my last letter appears to have given you such offence. If you think about the subject of our disagreement fairly, I think you must see I can only act in the way my Institute directs, and no matter how desirable it is for me to keep in your good books, I am obliged to follow the rules of my profession. Not to do so would only lead to a damaging of the relationship which we, as a profession, think is in the employer's best interests.

It is not possible for me at this stage to make a very accurate assessment of my expenses on this job, but a forecast based on the information now in my possession is around £500.

Have a good trip.

Yours sincerely,

This is a dignified reply to a very irritable letter. It puts Turvy in his place and does not deviate from the letter of the law so far as Sooty is concerned. It should ensure that the proper charges are met, and should not detract from the chances of further work. Sooty has demonstrated he is incorruptible, a fact that cannot but help his prospects for more work, either for Rubicon or other clients who may hear the history of this affair. The entire sordid business of fees now falls to the luckless Draughtsman.

SUTTON TO DRAUGHTSMAN (PERSONAL)

Dear Mr. Draughtsman, 20.5.70

LABWELS – Fees

I believe that during his absence George Turvy has turned over to you the rather embarrassing question of my last fee account. In particular, he seems to be objecting to my claim for a higher scale where alteration work is involved, and also in relation to out-of-pocket expenses which I have not so far claimed, but which I expect to be around £500 or a half of 1% of the value of the contract.

The whole thing amounts to about £800 which represents roughly only about 12% of my basic fee. I really cannot understand what it is that Mr. Turvy finds so unacceptable about this. It occurs on every job an architect has to do, and is less than the amount one would have to pay to borrow money these days. Furthermore, as I have tried to explain, there is nothing I can do about it, without breaking my Code of Conduct, which I am not prepared to do. If I were so prepared you *would* have reason for disquiet, for a man who will break one law is just as likely to break another, and that road can lead to disaster.

I do hope we can quickly reach an agreement.

Yours sincerely,

SUTTON TO THE SECRETARY, RIBA

Dear Mr. Secretary, 20.5.70

I have a problem with a client who seems unwilling to pay the higher rate for work to an existing building and to meet my out-of-pocket expenses. I have tried to explain the matter of my obligation to maintain the whole principle of the basis of our fees, but I only seem to have succeeded in making him more angry. I enclose a copy of the correspondence so far, and I would be grateful for your professional advice on how to proceed from here. I am sure I need not draw your attention to the fact these are my best clients and that I would be most unhappy to lose them.

Yours faithfully,

Whether the Secretary of the RIBA will feel able to come to Sutton's assistance is doubtful. The general attitude of the RIBA will probably be that it is there to make the rules, but it is up to members themselves to see they are upheld. It might have been better if Sutton had approached his Area Secretary first, because matters of this sort are usually dealt with at this level, where there is a more intimate knowledge of local affairs. However, there are some architects who would avoid this, as they would not want their affairs to be discussed by their close colleagues. On this occasion, however, it seemed the RIBA was prepared to intervene direct.

DAVID BLORE OBE MC MA (CANTAB) TO SUTTON

Dear Mr. Sutton, 24.5.70

Thank you for your letter concerning the problems you are having with the question of fees for alteration work and out-of-pocket expenses. It would have been more usual for you to have approached your Regional Chairman who, I am sure, would have been willing to help, but there is an important question of principle involved here, and I think we would be willing to directly intervene.

In the first instance I must have a word with the Chairman and Secretary of the Practice Committee and I will get in touch again when I have done so. As they are both in London at the moment, the process should not take too long.

I, of course, appreciate the sensitive position you are in as regards your future relations with a valued client and I have noted from the correspondence enclosed with your letter that any formal communication we might send to Rubicon should be addressed to Leslie Draughtsman.

Yours sincerely,

BLORE TO RUBICON

Dear Sir, 28.5.70

Confidential: For the attention of Mr. L. Draughtsman

One of our members, Mr. R. J. Sutton, has requested our assistance in the matter of a dispute over fees on a current project he is handling for you. I am writing on the direction of the Chairman and Honorary Secretary of our Practice Committee after discussing the matter with them.

It is perhaps not always realised that the current fee scale is both mandatory and minimum. It is not a maximum scale but in practice it usually works that way. There is a separate scale for work to existing buildings simply because, as a rule, the architect is involved in more work in relation to the overall cost of the job than he is when dealing with new work. If this arrangement did not exist, many architects would find themselves well out of pocket on such jobs and might not wish to repeat the experience. This would then be to the disadvantage of potential employers.

The Code also clearly states the rules on the payment of expenses. You may well feel this is a matter that concerns only you and your architect, but this is not so. If he could not reach agreement with you he had little alternative but to seek our assistance. He is bound to uphold the Code, and if he did not do so he could find himself in trouble with the Discipline Committee of the Institute. He has given us a copy of the disputed account and we find nothing out of order in it.

In writing to you we are trying to be helpful. A dispute of this kind is damaging both the architect and his employer. All we are doing is to point out that Mr. Sutton has no other option than to act as he has done. If you can be convinced of that, perhaps you can accept the situation and agree to meet his rightful costs. If you cannot please do not hesitate to continue this correspondence. We are always prepared to continue to seek agreement in the interest of our members and their clients.

Yours faithfully,

DRAUGHTSMAN TO BLORE

Dear Mr. Blore,

Thank you for your letter of the 28th May. It will be helpful to me in trying to explain to my management that the situation is as you state. As you rightly say, this is not always realised.

I understand from Mr. Sutton that he has been sent a copy of your letter. I hope to resolve this unhappy affair as soon as possible and I will reply to you when I have something to report.

Yours sincerely,

DRAUGHTSMAN TO SUTTON (CONFIDENTIAL)

Dear Mr. Sutton, 4.6.70

LABWELS – Fees

As you are probably aware, I have had a letter from the RIBA about the question of your fees and expenses. The letter makes it quite clear that we have to accept your account and that you have no other course than to insist upon this.

In the light of the RIBA's remarks I discussed the matter with J. J. Boffin, our Managing Director. Although Mr. Boffin was also a little disappointed that these costs should appear so soon after the rights of light business, he told me that your account should immediately be met in full. I have written to Mr. Blore of the RIBA to inform him of this and I think you will find the matter has now been settled satisfactorily.

Yours sincerely,

SUTTON TO DRAUGHTSMAN (PERSONAL)

Dear Leslie, 6.6.70

LABWELS – Fees

Many thanks for your letter. I really am grateful for your help in sorting out this wretched affair. I must try to avoid treading on your management's toes again and as far as possible, I will try to do everything through you and avoid bringing them in unless it is absolutely essential. You, of course' will have to be the judge of that. Again, my thanks.

Yours sincerely,

TURVY TO SUTTON

Dear Richard, 6.6.70

I felt I should have the decency to drop you a line to apologise for my extreme irritability over the question of your fees. As you may have gathered, I had rather a lot on my plate during the lead-up to the Tokyo trip and I'm afraid I lost my sense of proportion over one or two innocuous matters. I gather from Draughtsman that he managed to sort it out and I'm sorry if I put you to any needless inconvenience.

The purpose of this letter is also to give you some welcome news on the interior design front. When I got back I was surprised to find there have been some mysterious moves among the merchant princes in the City and that the Chairmanship of this company has passed from Sir Isaac Gildenstein to one Sir Sidney Rough. I gather the new man has no time for frills and has expressed complete indifference as to what we do with our Chairman's Dining Room. J. J. Boffin has therefore decided to give you a free hand in the design of the interior, subject, that is, to his approval before any actual order is placed.

I believe you have a scheme of your own on the stocks and if you would like to drop in for a drink one evening this week, J.J. and I would like to take a look at it. Ring me first.

Yours,

It is not unusual in the City of London for the lords of finance to acquire and discard Chairmanships like clothes. In this case, Sir Isaac's brilliant move has also wafted Sutton from the realm of Adam ceilings to that of superior contract furnishing. Sutton's scheme is apparently approved, because we hear no more about it.

20

Screeds and Settlement

DRAUGHTSMAN TO SUTTON

Dear Richard, 10.4.70

LABWELS

I am not sure when you made your last site visit, but Harris has drawn my attention to certain cracks in the screeds, some only hairline but some more serious. As you know, we have three types of floor finish, all of which are due to start on site in the near future, and if there are any serious problems it is best that we know about them before flooring work commences. Would you please have a look at these and arrange a date when we can make a joint visit, perhaps with the builder to decide what, if anything, is to be done?

Yours sincerely,

MEMORANDUM 10.4.70

From Henry Higgins
To R. S. J. Sutton
Job LABWELS

You will remember that you gave me a special duty to see to it that the screeds were laid strictly in accordance with the specification. I have taken this to include keeping an eye on them afterwards and have made a visual inspection once a week. I believe Bomber Harris has also kept a close watch although he does that with everything.

Until recently, everything seemed to being going well. K & B kept them damp for the appropriate period and apart from the episode with the gas driers there seemed no reason to expect any trouble. In the last few weeks, however, some cracking has developed. Nothing very much except for one particular case, but some are a bit more than what I should call hairline cracks, although there does not seem to be any hollowness.

On the ground floor we have had the asphalt sub-floor down for several weeks now and yesterday I made a careful inspection of this and I'm afraid found some haircracks in that. Toughgrain Floors Ltd. are due on site next week to start on both the cork and woodblock floors, and I think we should decide now whether or not they will have to be delayed.

K & B TO SUTTON

Dear Sir, 10.4.70

Rubicon LABWELS

Messrs. Toughgrain Floors Ltd. are due on site next week to make a start on the woodblock and corktile floors, starting on the ground floor where there is an asphalt subfloor. We always like to satisfy ourselves before hand that everything is in order for the arrival of a new sub-contractor on site and, accordingly, Mr. Steele made an inspection of screeds and asphalt. To our disappointment we found that some cracks had developed, but then in our experience this is virtually inevitable, and so far as we can tell by tapping there are no hollow patches below the screeds. There is one place where the cracking is much worse than elsewhere and we would like you to see this.

Mr. Harris has also drawn our attention to the matter and we think it is important to meet you on the site this week, to check the situation and decide whether the flooring contractor should be put off for the time being.

Yours faithfully,

Alarm bells ringing from three directions at once. We can envisage Sutton sitting with his hands over his ears. Here are the makings of a brass-bound, copper-bottomed, pig's breakfast. We have involved the main contractor, CBP Ltd., the asphalters, plasterers and possibly flooring contractors. There is no time to be lost. The site meeting took place with notes taken by HH as below.

NOTES OF A SITE MEETING HELD ON 14.4.70

Present:	L. Draughtsman	Rubicon Ltd.
	R. Harris	Rubicon Ltd.
	A. Steele	Knott & Bannister
	B. Bunter	Plasterer foreman
	R. J. Sutton	Architect
	H. Higgins	Architect

1. A tour of the screeds and asphalt was made and the following points noted:

1.1 At first-floor level the cracks were mainly hairline, although it could not be said with certainty that they had finished developing. Tapping revealed no hollowness.

1.2 At positions over the main beams the cracks appeared wider and to follow loosely the line of the beams, although this was not universal.

1.3 At ground-floor level all screeds have been covered by the asphalt sub-floor which was examined and some fine cracks were found, but not to the same extent as in the screeds.

2. At the junction between the third and fourth bays from the north there was quite a major crack at both floor levels and unlike all the other cracks there was lipping, i.e. the floor surface on one side, (the north) was about 8 mm above the other. Some diagonal sheer cracks also appeared in the wall plaster.

3. Following the inspection a discussion took place to decide what action must now be taken to meet these problems. RJS said we could not possibly consider the matter calmly while expecting the imminent arrival of the flooring contractor and that inevitably they would have to be postponed. Mr. Steele would deal with that immediately, though it was recognised that other problems might arise out of this action. Mr. Harris took the chance to point out that, as far as he was concerned, this would not be accepted as an official reason for delay in the completion date. He based this on the idea that once a main contractor took over a site the responsibility for seeing that all sub-contractors met their dates, and for overcoming site problems lay with him (the builder) and that no * * * * excuses would be accepted. There was no response.

4. K & B were to take up the question of the asphalt with Tarrag and with the flooring contractor.

5. The cracks at beam positions at first-floor level are to be cut out for the architect's inspection.

SUTTON TO THE CORKSCREW BAR CO. LTD.

Dear Sirs, 14.4.70

Rubicon Ltd. LABWELS Building

You will recollect that in order to overcome a time-delay problem on this job, we abandoned, at your suggestion, the original cast in-situ floors, for your system using precast concrete beams. These were also prestressed, a situation I am never very happy with, but 'needs must when the Devil drives', as he did in this case. At the time, I stressed to the builder the importance of seeing that the continuity steel above beam positions was well and truly inserted.

It seems my worst fears have been realised. Recently cracks have been noted above beam positions in the screed. I have had these cut out and find that the continuity steel is both too short to develop full bond stress and too near to the surface. The result is that it has failed.

At first sight this failure might seem to be of small importance as the prestressed beams are probably safe over the span without continuity. That is for you to say. They will, however, obviously have deflected more that they should and this could have its affect on the screeds above.

It is essential that remedial work should commence immediately. The job is already partially stopped, and any extensive further delay would be very serious. In my opinion what seems to be needed is some form of support at the centre of each span. This would take out some of the deflection whilst the concrete between the prestressed beams is cut back, new longer continuity bars inserted lower down than before and new concrete cast. I am not, however, trying to tell you what needs to be done. As designers of the floors as well as erectors, I am sure I need not remind you that you have full responsibility for producing a satisfactory floor, which we certainly do not have at the moment.

I look forward to having your proposals immediately, together with a date when you can move on to site and an assessment how long the work will take.

Yours faithfully,

Sutton seems to know his structural principles in the field of R C Concrete in its various forms. This being so, he cannot resist the temptation to teach his grandmother to suck eggs. He would really have been better advised to just say, 'put it right'. On the other hand Corkscrew will know that they are not going to be able to blind anyone with science.

It is a nasty situation and one Sutton doesn't deserve since he did stress the importance of what was not done. Corkscrew realise they have dropped an outsize clanger and reply immediately.

CORKSCREW BAR CO. TO SUTTON

Dear Sir, 17.4.70

Rubicon Ltd. LABWELS Building

We have your letter and have taken immediate action. Our engineer was on site yesterday and we have already produced a drawing for the remedial work. A copy is enclosed. We have all the material needed in stock, except for scaffold jacks which we can hire in Winterfield.

As we see it, the site operation could be completed in four days and to avoid any interference with other trades, we could do this during the next two weekends. This will mean that our centre-span scaffold will be in position over half the ground-floor area for two weeks, but suitable phasing of the flooring work should avoid any serious difficulty.

We are sorry that you have been put to this inconvenience because of sub-standard workmanship on our part, but we do assure you that this is the exception, not the rule, with this type of construction which you regard with some dubiety.

Yours faithfully,

Here we have a firm that takes its responsibilities seriously, and is pulling out all the stops to get its reputation back. The odds are that, at the end of the day, Sutton will remember them more kindly than if there had been no problem at all. They have also found something else.

CORKSCREW BAR CO. TO SUTTON

Dear Sir, 18.4.70

Rubicon LABWELS

Further to our letter of yesterday we acknowledge your telephone instruction to proceed on the lines outlined in our last letter. Unfortunately, there is another matter of the same kind, which our engineer noticed whilst on site.

The crack which appears between the 3rd and 4th bays from the North is not typical. It is both greater and there is lipping of about 8 mm, the North side being the higher. We expect you will have noticed this, and we wonder whether you have divined the obvious cause? You will recollect the business we had with the foundations which was dealt with by your Mr. Higgins whilst you were on holiday last year. It was finally resolved by the use of lined piles designed and placed by Uriah Heap Ltd. We designed and placed the pile caps and beams in lieu of the original loadbearing footings which were still retained over 70% of the site.

As this crack appears at the junction between the two types of foundations, it is clearly the result of differential settlement. The piles, bearing as they do on solid boulder clay way below the level where there could be any kind of shrinkage or movement, have remained stationary. Elsewhere on the site there has been a settlement of about 8 mm, something quite normal and unimportant if the whole building settles together, but clearly noticable in this case.

Differential settlement is a well-known hazard in buildings where more than one foundation system is used. Unfortunately, we were not consulted at the time of the decision to use piles to overcome the running sand problem, otherwise we would have advised against it. As things now stand, however, we are prepared to advise you as to how, in our opinion, this problem may be best overcome.

Yours faithfully,

This is all very true, but at the time the problem arose, Corkscrew Bar were well acquainted with all the relevant facts, because they had to redesign part of their own reinforcement to accommodate the use of piles. They made no mention of their concern at the time. This is one of those situations where the difference between having parts of a structure designed by a sub-contractor, as opposed to a consulting engineer, shows up to the disadvantage of the former.

Had the foundation design been done by a consultant there is no doubt that the possible problems of differential settlement would have been highlighted and settled at that time. However, it is the client who is usually shy of appointing consultants, mainly because it is another fee, and it is difficult to prove that the consultant easily saves his fee in the cost of the work on site. As there is no consultant, Sutton accepts the offer of help from Corkscrew.

SUTTON TO CORKSCREW BAR CO.

Dear Sirs, 20.4.70

Thank you for your letter. I am surprised to hear at this stage that you anticipated trouble from differential settlement at the time the decision was taken to use piles. If so, it was surely your duty to inform me at the time. As you know, you were in effect in the position of consulting engineer as far as the design of the foundations was concerned, and there was no other source of advice available to me at the time.

Having said this, I would be grateful for your expert advice on how best to deal with the situation, now it has unfortunately arisen.

Yours faithfully,

This may sound a bit churlish, but it does describe the position that Sutton finds himself in quite well. Reinforcement suppliers, steelwork suppliers, and others in similar specialist situations, have all developed design and supply organisations, to help sell their product, which is of course their main concern. There is nothing wrong with the ability of these departments to design sound structures. Indeed, they may sometimes claim, with justice, a certain expertise in their own specialist field. They are fond of claiming to architects that they save the cost of a consultant's fee, and the client is always very willing to listen to this point of view. In fact, this is not really true since the cost of the design has to be found somewhere, and the answer is that it lies within the overall cost of the material being supplied and fixed. Theoretically, therefore, it should cost no more in total to employ a consultant, but some of the suppliers will tell you, they do not alter the rates they use for pricing the material when using a consultant's design, because they still have to do most of the drawings anyway. They will also claim that in the event of anything going wrong they are in a much better position than a consultant, with their vast capital resources, to meet the costs involved. In effect they are their own professional insurers. What they do not mention is that the weight of those resources might be used against the architect rather than for him.

Over the last 20 years or so there has been increasing resort to the services of consultants and most Government departments and Local Authorities now insist upon it. The exception is probably the large industrial corporations which consider their own engineering staff can provide the services normally supplied by a consultant.

CORKSCREW BAR CO. TO SUTTON

Dear Sir, 21.4.70

Rubicon LABWELS

Thank you for your letter. Firstly, we should say that we have never laid claim to providing the same services as a consultant. If we did our prices would not be competitive.

Reverting to your problem with differential settlement, we would expect that at this stage at LABWELS approximately 70% of the total settlement we can expect has by now taken place. As this is about 8 mm, we can expect a further 3 mm, which might, however, not fully develop for the next two or three years.

When we redesigned the foundations we did separate those on piles from the normal loadbearing bases, so that they could move independently without distorting the structure. It is therefore only the question of the finishes which needs to be dealt with. We suggest that the screeds at each side of the joint be cut back and refinished up to an L-shaped metal stop at each side with the L's back-to-back so they can move independently without causing cracks.

The same system on the same line can be used for the plastered walls. If there is to be a partition on this line nothing further will be required. If not, observation will reveal when the extent of the settlement has been reached, when the two levels can be gently graded into each other. The difference in level can only be slight because when the insertion of the L-shaped stops is done the existing 8 mm difference will be taken out.

If there is anything on which you have further queries please do not hesitate to contact us.

Yours faithfully,

This all sounds very straightforward, but Corescrew have missed a point, because next we read:

CORKSCREW BAR CO. TO SUTTON

Dear Sir, 22.4.70

Rubicon LABWELS

In our letter of yesterday we omitted to draw your attention to a difference in the circumstances at ground and first-floor level. At ground level the floor slab is supported from the two types of foundation structure and separated by building paper. Thus the difference in settlement is directly represented by the lipping at that point. At first floor however, there is, or should have been, continuity so there should have been bending rather than lipping. The poor standard of continuity which we are now correcting did, however, allow a degree of shear movement but less than that at ground floor.

The effect of this is that there will be some small difference in level between the 4th and 5th frames which could cause distortion in the brick and block spandrels below and between windows. If you inspect these you will find there is some stepped cracking both outside and inside which is typical of these conditions. We believe these panels will have to be rebuilt and if this is done now (as we expect it must be) expansion joints at the positions marked on the enclosed drawing should be incorporated to ensure there are no further cracks due to further movement.

There will also be some small degree of strain on the longitudinal members of the steel frame, but this is small enough to be ignored.

We trust you will find these comments useful.

Yours faithfully,

No doubt Sutton will. He would have found them much more useful if they had been made at the time the foundations were being constructed. He is now once again in that annoying dilemma of whether to report this situation in detail to his client with some idea of the extra cost involved, or simply carry on as though nothing significant had happened, and that the episode comes within the category of minor troubles which are inevitably part of any building contract. If Sutton had a more reasonably sized contingency fund he could afford to take that attitude. Another problem is that the trouble has been well publicised and both Draughtsman and Harris know about it. He decides to appeal to Draughtsman.

SUTTON TO DRAUGHTSMAN

Dear Leslie, 24.4.70

LABWELS

The problems with the screeds, settlement and structural continuity have now been sorted out, but it must be obvious to everyone that the remedial work is going to involve some extra cost. There are several people or firms who could be held at least partially responsible for such costs, but past experience has taught me that they may well try to disclaim responsibility and lay the blame elsewhere.

I write to ask whether you think this is a case that should be specifically reported to your management with some guess (that is all it could be) as to the extra cost? Or could we treat it as one of those routine incidents which occur on every job?

Yours sincerely,

Events of this type, routine or not, are the very devil to sort out. The situation involves a number of different firms each of which is reliant to some extent on the quality of the work of another party, over which they have had no control. Main contractors are used to this situation, but they have a weapon in the shape of future possible work which they can wield to good effect. The sub-contractors themselves have no such influence and are going to protest strongly against being lumbered with anything which is not their own direct responsibility.

Experienced architects all know about this and try to avoid setting up arrangements which allow such situations to occur. Sutton is not yet quite in that category.

K & B TO SUTTON

Dear Sir, 24.4.70

LABWELS

At the meeting we had on site recently to deal with the problems of screeds etc., we were left with the job of contacting Tarrag Ltd. about minor cracks in the asphalt sub-floor. We enclose a copy of their letter and would be pleased to receive your instructions re same.

TARRAG LTD. TO K & B (COPY)

Yours faithfully,

Dear Sirs, 22.4.70

We have your letter re the sub-floor we laid at the LABWELS building. The hair cracks you observed are of only minor significance. They would not normally occur in roofing asphalt, but for floors we use a mix which sets a little harder to give a good firm base for the finish. This is not in itself shrinkable, but if laid on a screed which shrinks can move with it. In fact, it is separated from the screed by a membrane, but it would appear that in this case, this has not prevented adherence to the screed completely.

We will send a man down who should be able to seal any hair cracks in one morning, following which, you may happily proceed with floor-laying. We shall have a man in your area next week and he will attend to it.

Yours faithfully,

SUTTON TO K & B

Dear Sirs, 27.4.70

LABWELS

Thank you for your letter. It seems that we do not really have a problem with the asphalt sub-floors. This means you can allow Toughgrain Floors Ltd. on to the site as soon as Tarrag's man has finished, so the delay should not exceed about a week. While Toughgrain are working on the asphalt sub-floor, the remedial work on the first floor should be drying out enough to let them proceed to the first floor without a break.

Please instruct Toughgrain accordingly,

Yours faithfully,

Sutton has got it wrong. Toughgrain are not doing the first floor which is a type of finish they do not handle. A lapse of this kind usually indicates overwork probably combined with other worries. He will have to watch himself. Cases of nervous breakdown are not uncommon and the architectural profession has a higher suicide rate than many others.

DRAUGHTSMAN TO SUTTON

Dear Richard, 27.4.70

LABWELS

I have given some thought to your letter and have had a word with Harris about it. You may be surprised to learn that he had already defined the matter in his own mind as routine, something one can expect on any job. He sees no reason to make a fuss about it, quite the reverse. His comment was, 'Don't tell those chairborne * * * * anything about it or we shall be * * * * about forever until they make up their * * * * minds. I'll stand by you if there's any comeback later.'

I am inclined to agree with him. After all, we are supposed to be here to deal with problems, so I suggest we forget it for the time being.

Yours sincerely,

Harris clearly has some positive abilities or despite his history, he would not have lasted so long. Despite his blustery exterior he is a man of principle and that principle is to get on with the job and to hell with anyone who might slow it down. He is also not afraid to stand by his decisions. In fact, he is probably not afraid of anything or anyone.

K & B TO SUTTON

Dear Sir, 30.4.70

LABWELS

Thank you for your letter. Tarrag's man came as promised and Toughgrain Floors made a start the same day. We think that between us we have kept any bad effects of this awkward business to the minimum.

In your letter you mention the question of Toughgrain Floors moving up to first floor, and we should remind you that the upper-storey finishes are, in fact, to be laid by Shefleford Ceramics who are also appointed for the lab. bench top tiling.

Yours faithfully,

21

Sutton's Double Date

McDONALD TO SUTTON

Dear Sooty, 1.7.70

Project 752 at Pwlys Rhonda

As I told you on the telephone last week we are to build a new plant in south Wales designated as above. We shall be doing most of the engineering ourselves, but we have not got the spare capacity to tackle the ancillary buildings and I would like you to handle these for us if you can. I realise it is a long way to travel and that we should perhaps consider using a local firm of architects. However, there is probably more advantage in having your architect close by during the design stages than during site construction. At that stage we will in any case have our own supervisory staff on the site and visits at two or three week intervals by you or your rep. should be all that is needed.

I have spoken to the chief (Philip Brunel) about this and he agrees. 'Better the devil you know' was his comment. Architects are not his favourite kind of people.

There is to be a meeting in Bristol where we have acquired temporary offices for the project team. Jim Bracewell will be i/c the work you will be designing. I think you will remember him from your days here. He will be there and the general idea is for everyone to throw bricks at the outline programme until they have knocked it into a more realistic shape. Our friends from across the Atlantic will be there too, so we can expect a few sparks. If you can make it, it would be best for you to be there for the two days 27th, 28th of this month, but the first day may be enough. If you wish, we could travel together, in either your car or mine.

Let me know what you think.

Yours aye,

Although we don't know what size this new job is, it sounds promising. It is also likely to stretch Sutton's organisation to the limit when it really gets going. Usually there is a period of a few months during which the bare bones of a scheme are put together and there are not a lot of man hours involved, but it looks as though Sutton should be making plans for expansion, not always easy to achieve in busy times. It is in the nature of things that when times are slack there always seems to be good staff seeking new places, but when times are brisk they disappear as though by magic.

SUTTON TO McDONALD

Dear Ian, 3.7.70

Project 752 at Pwlys Rhonda

Many thanks for your letter. I am naturally delighted to be asked to handle the architectural part of this project for you and, if possible, I would like to meet for a drink to discuss the thing in outline before the Bristol meeting. I can then make a reasonable cockshy at how much is involved for me and how I can cope, especially with the possibility of extra staff being needed. I do remember Bracewell – a bit of an old stick-in-the-mud if I remember rightly, but essentially a nice guy and someone I would enjoy working with.

As regards the journey, much as I would value your company, I have things to do in London at that time and it would suit me to go that way. In any case, I do prefer the train which seems about the only place one can relax these days, so if you have no objection I will see you in Bristol on the 27th. No doubt you will let me have full details before then, and a date and time when we can meet.

Yours sincerely,

TURVY TO SUTTON

Dear Richard, 3.7.70

LABWELS

Our new chairman is due to spend a few days with us at the end of the month. He wishes to review what we might call 'the state of the nation', including all current building projects and in particular, the cost of these.

As you know to your benefit, we have not had Sir Sidney long and naturally we are anxious he should get a good impression of the Company in general. We shall have our own senior design staff available to discuss the projects they are handling, and you should be available to answer queries on the two buildings you currently have in hand. I cannot give you exact details at the moment, but you should keep free the 27th, 28th and 29th of this month.

Yours sincerely,

That's life. These are possibly the two most important events in the development of Sutton's practice and they clash head on. What should he do? Neither party are going to be happy with Henry Higgins, stalwart though he may be. It is a situation which might well lead Sooty to think about taking a partner, if he has not already done so. Single partner practices (if this is not a contradiction in terms) are particularly vulnerable to this kind of difficulty, together with a lot of others; illness and holidays to name but two. Of course, they also have their advantages, especially if they can rely on the services of a good, sound, loyal qualified assistant. Turvy is not going to like the following reply:

SUTTON TO TURVY

Dear George, 5.7.70

Thank you for your letter about Sir Sidney's projected visit at the end of this month. It is a very awkward coincidence but unfortunately, the dates you mention clash with an equally important visit I have already agreed to make to Leverpullers at Bristol. As I have already confirmed I will attend, I'm afraid it would be impossible for me to back out now. It seems, therefore, I have no alternative but to make my apologies to your Chairman for being unable to meet him during his visit to Winterfield on this occasion.

I wonder if I could suggest any useful alternative? My assistant Henry Higgins could attend in my place as he knows the job well enough and is a very able young man. Alternatively, I will be in London myself for a couple of days after my trip to Bristol and if Sir Sidney is back from Winterfield by then, I could call at his office to fill him in about anything he wishes to know about my projects. I would willingly do this if you think it would help.

Yours sincerely,

Well put. When two appointments clash there is only one honourable way to proceed and that is to keep the first. Clearly there are situations where the relative importance of the two meetings will overthrow this rule, but in this case, that is not so. Hard though it may be for Turvy to accept, Sutton's date with Leverpullers is probably the more important of the two.

TURVY TO SUTTON

Dear Richard, 6.7.70

I was very concerned to read your last letter saying you cannot be present at our Chairman's meetings because of a prior engagement. I was firmly of the opinion that we were your most important clients and we were to be treated accordingly, whenever priorities arose.

I am sorry to say that a visit from the excellent Higgins will not be sufficient on this occasion, nor will calling on Sir Sidney in London. I really feel you must try to make new arrangements with Leverpullers and be here as requested.

Yours sincerely,

SUTTON TO McDONALD

Dear Ian, 8.7.70

Project 752 at Pwlys Rhonda

I am very sorry to say a problem has blown up over the dates of my intended visit to Bristol. I believe you want me at Bristol on 27th and 28th and, unfortunately, Rubicon also want me to be available at Winterfield for a meeting with their new Chairman, Sir Sidney Rough, on the same dates. My appointments with you were made first and so I naturally regarded myself as unavailable to Rubicon. Unfortunately, George Turvy, who in effect is my master there, took this very badly and is insisting that I ditch you to attend his meetings. As my relations with him have been rather strained recently over one or two matters, I suppose there is no faint possibility that the dates of the Bristol meeting could be changed?

Yours,

McDONALD TO SUTTON

Dear Sooty, 9.7.70

Much as I would love to oblige you, I'm afraid the dates of the Bristol meeting must stay as they are. However, 'nil desperandum' as I think we can help. I have had a word with our chief, PB, who thinks that Rubicon's new boss is a chap called Sidney Rough. If so, he knows him from way back and he is going to have a word to see if you could meet Rough in London.

Let's hope PB is successful and, if he is, I look forward to seeing you in Bristol. Perhaps we could have a night out on the town?

Yours aye,

It is nice to have friends in the right places. One of the compensations of growing old is that one finds one's friends have somehow become important and influential people.

SIR SIDNEY ROUGH TO TURVY (COPY)

Dear Turvy,

Forthcoming meeting at Winterfield

I had a call from an old college friend the other day, one Philip Brunel, who it appears is now Chief Engineer to Liver-pullers, Bristol. It seems that we are both currently employing a young architect called Richard Sutton who used at one time to work in Brunel's department.

I expect you will know that the dates for our meetings at Winterfield clash with those for a project conference that Leverpullers are having at Bristol to launch a new project in that area. Apparently we are both expecting Sutton to be there.

I gather Sutton is a one-man band and we cannot expect the poor fellow to cut himself in half. Brunel says his presence is important to them, whereas I cannot really say the same for us. As you may be aware, I do not interest myself in the type of buildings you currently have underway at Winterfield. Indeed, I regard them as an unfortunate necessity. All I want is a reasonable forecast of what the costs are going to be and I am sure you can have that available for my visit.

If I have time perhaps I will meet Sutton on some other trip to Winterfield. In the meantime, I look forward to meeting you on the 27th.

Yours sincerely,

SUTTON TO TURVY

Dear George, 16.7.70

Chairman's Visit

Further to your telephone call, this letter is to confirm that as I will not now be attending your meetings on the 27th and 28th I shall prepare, with the help of James le Mesurier, a statement of the anticipated final cost of both buildings in the light of the latest information we have available. The resulting costs should be pretty close to actuality.

I must say once again how sorry I am not to be able to present the figures in person, but it was very kind of your Chairman to take it the way he did. Thank you for the copy of his letter.

Yours sincerely,

If this batch of correspondence has any lessons for us it is the fact there are some clients like George Turvy who develop a kind of proprietory interest in their architect, to the extent they resent him working for anyone else. This can make life very difficult and there may come a stage when the architect simply has to say, 'Look! I'm a private practitioner and much as I enjoy working for you, I need work from other sources if I am to survive.' An architect only develops his full potential if he is involved in a wide variety of projects and it is in the best interests of all his clients that he should do so.

22

Grousing and Grinding

SUTTON TO SHEFLEFORD CERAMICS

Dear Sirs, 24.4.70

Rubicon Ltd. LABWELS Building

In the past my clients have always used the traditional

Accrington red ceramic tiles for their bench-top work where the surface has to be acid resisting. I have, however, mentioned to them that there is now a much wider selection of fully-fired acid-proof tiles available in a number of colours and surface designs. I understand these are at least equal to, if not better than, the standard red, in terms of chemical resistance and hardness.

I would be pleased to have your alternative quotation for the use of Smörgesbad flamed tiles, which I gather you can have from stock in lieu of the standard reds.

Yours faithfully,

SHEFLEFORD CERAMICS TO SUTTON

Dear Sir, 26.4.70

Rubicon LABWELS

Thank you for your letter. Our price for using the Smörgesbad tiles will be £1,450.00 an increase of £350 on our original quotation which we think should be well worthwhile.

At the same time, we should point out that the technique of laying such tiles is quite different, since we do not use a cement-based mortar, but one of the new mastic compounds, which are a good deal better in terms of acid and other chemical resistance. The technique involves a thin bed and comparatively wide joints since the mastic cannot be compressed into a very thin joint and gaps would ensue.

If you wish, we could do a sample square yard or so for your client's inspection. Alternatively, they could look at a job we have recently finished at Wigburn which we think looks very attractive.

We await your instructions.

Yours faithfully,

Rubicon have always admitted that they do not care to be guinea pigs and tend to steer clear of new methods. Sutton has accordingly moved with some circumspection and there have clearly been a number of telephone calls leading up to the following letter.

TURVY TO SUTTON

Dear Richard, 28.4.70

LABWELS Bench-top tiling

I am sorry to say that I am jumping in on this question of

tiling, since I have heard from Dr. Science that you have suggestions for bench tiling which will look more attractive than the old red Accringtons. We must remember, however, that these tiles have an important job to perform – a job that the Accringtons have always done very well.

I am prepared to believe that the Swedes know more about ceramics than we do and that their tiles are to all intents and purposes perfect, but what I cannot accept is that we should have joints $\frac{3}{16}$″ to $\frac{1}{4}$″ wide. As I have always understood, it is in the joints where any weakness is likely to be and so logically speaking, they must be kept to the barest possible minimum, which we have always regarded as $\frac{1}{16}$″.

I'm afraid the suggestion as it stands would be unacceptable to us and I feel Shefleford Ceramics must be made to think again about tiling with very fine joints. As I am shortly leaving on a business trip, I would be obliged if you could get this matter settled without delay.

Yours sincerely,

That doesn't leave much room for manoeuvre. It is clear that Sutton has had Shefleford down on the site to talk direct to Rubicon, but this doesn't seem to have made any difference. 'There's none so blind as them that will not see'. Shefleford lay it on the line.

SHEFLEFORD TO SUTTON

Dear Sir, 30.4.70

Rubicon LABWELS

We confirm the result of our discussions on the site with yourself and your clients re bench-top tiling.

We still maintain that the Swedish tile would make a better and a nicer job but we are only prepared to lay it in accordance with the maker's instructions and our own past experience. To try to lay this tile thin-bed *and* with thin joints would surely lead to trouble. Your clients do not seem to realise that this is not a thick-bed on concrete job and that the benches are now all made.

In our view there is only one way to provide what they want at this stage and that is to use red Accringtons, which we can get at $\frac{3}{8}$, leaving us with a thicker bed which will allow of using an acid-resistant cement and silver sand as a bedding and

"Harris had a go himself, and could do no better."

jointing compound with which we ought to be able to get down to $\frac{1}{16}''$ joints.

As we are ready to start, we would appreciate your decision at the earliest opportunity.

Yours faithfully,

SUTTON TO SHEFLEFORD

Dear Sirs, 2.5.70

LABWELS Bench Tops

Please proceed with Accrington $\frac{3}{8}$ on cement bed, with narrow joints as in your letter of 30.4.70.

Yours faithfully,

Shefleford seem to have moved in straight away, but we are not yet out of the wood. Bench-tops are something about which everyone at Rubicon are fanatical. You will find them going over each new surface with straight edge and level looking for lipping and hollow or proud surfaces. Any laid to falls are even more closely examined. After a break of about two weeks we find:

DRAUGHTSMAN TO SUTTON

Dear Richard, 16.5.70

LABWELS Bench tiling

I can see serious trouble ahead with this tiling. I wish you would come over and have a look at it with Harris and myself. We are not at all happy and I know this goes for quite a few people who pull a heavier punch than I do.

The thing is that they are not getting the surface really level and true. Harris has had a word with the foreman (and not in his usual way, as he can be helpful when he tries). We suspect the trouble lies mainly in the tiles themselves which are not all perfectly true to size and some have a slight camber. You would not notice this with the eye alone until they are fixed in place. Shefleford's men are trying to select, but it is not easy and they are going to have a lot left over. I think we are going to have to say something before they get any further. At the moment they have done about 10% of the job.

Yours sincerely,

NOTES MADE FOLLOWING A SITE MEETING AT 11 A.M. ON 18.5.70 TO CONSIDER THE PROBLEM OF THE TILED BENCH TOPS

Present:	L. Draughtsman	Rubicon
	R. Harris	Rubicon
	J. Clayman	Shefleford Ceramics
	R. Sutton	Architect
	H. Higgins	Architect

1. The work completed to date was examined and checked in a number of places with straight-edge and level. Superficially, the work looked satisfactory but lipping was found to occur almost to the thickness of a sixpenny piece and the top surface of some tiles was found to have a slight incline although overall the levels were as close as could be expected.

2. Clayman demonstrated his problems by laying a few tiles and it could be seen that even after selecting them carefully, there were places where these discrepancies seemed unavoidable. Harris, who was a first class bricky at one time, had a go himself and could do no better.

3. Draughtsman said he had already had Dr. Science leaning over his shoulder with a message that he is not going to accept them. He has had words with others in the management team at Winterfield and they stand together on this. If necessary, they will have the whole lot removed and bring in someone else. In that case, Shefleford would not get a penny and a very unpleasant situation could arise.

4. Asked what he thought was really the trouble, Clayman said that the Accrington tiles should never have been used on a bed only $\frac{3}{8}''$ thick with very fine joints. Unlike the newer fully-fired ceramics, the Accrington reds are not a perfect shape and some have a slight twist. It all arises out of the method of manufacture. However, laid in the usual way on a bed of say $\frac{3}{4}''$ sand cement and with an $\frac{1}{8}''$ joint, the small eccentricities are easy to lose. Even with narrower joints, by picking the tiles it is possible to get what looks like an *almost* perfect job. Clayman also said that in his view his boss should never have taken it on but he apparently doesn't like disappointing people.

5. It was agreed that I should get on to all concerned and try to define a policy.

Sooty decides that attack is the best form of defence and takes the battle into enemy territory before he has actually been attacked. This was undoubtedly the best policy.

SUTTON TO TURVY

Dear George, 19.5.70

LABWELS Bench tops

This unhappy history continued to unfold during your absence and I believe you are now as well acquainted with it as I am. I also understand that the work so far completed has been described as unacceptable. It seems that in trying to improve standards I have only succeeded in doing the reverse.

At first sight it seems difficult to understand how these problems could arise in a type of work which in the past apparently caused you no problems at all. I have made my own inspection in company with Draughtsman and Harris and have watched the difficulties with which these tilers are faced. Since then I have spoken to Norriman their MD (who is also a trade-tested tiler amongst other things) and he is coming to see me tomorrow. Shefleford whilst not a large firm, stick entirely to their own specialist field, and are reckoned to be about the best in the business. I gather from Norriman that he may have a solution and will let you know as soon as I have anything concrete to report.

Yours sincerely,

TURVY TO SUTTON

Dear Richard, 22.5.70

Thank you for your letter. It did not seem to contain much in the way of comfort. I really cannot understand how we have got into this sort of a mess about a process which seemed so simple before.

I think it would be good for your soul to have a look round some of the bench tiling we have had done in the past. Why not ask Leslie to show you round?

Yours sincerely,

NORRIMAN TO SUTTON

Dear Mr. Sutton, 22.5.70

Rubicon Bench Tiling

I was pleased to meet you yesterday and to discuss the

problem we have on this job. I may say I have done an awful lot of bench-top tiling in my time and never had a job with the problems that this one has. In a way it is my own fault as I should never have accepted instructions for what I knew could be difficult but one doesn't like to admit defeat.

I am aware that your clients are now regarding me as just a poor craftsman, because they cannot (or will not) see the difference between laying on concrete with a $\frac{3}{4}''+$ bed and working off a surface with only $\frac{3}{8}''$ to spare, using tiles which they imagine are true all through, but which in fact are nothing of the sort.

Looking at the job so far, it seems to me that the worst case of lipping that there is about $\frac{1}{16}''$, no more, and there are not a lot of those. This being so I can use grinders on the tops to remove the lipping and generally improve the flatness of the finished surface.

I realise you might be somewhat shocked by this suggestion, but I can assure you that when finished and finally polished you will not be able to distinguish between ground and unground tiles. The important thing is that these tiles are fired through and through and there is no surface patina with a softer body beneath. Such a tile would be quite unsuitable for this type of treatment.

We cannot start until we have had tiles laid for at least 2 weeks and it is going to be a long hard task, but I can guarantee the result. I should also say that although I do not regard myself as being entirely to blame for this situation, I will undertake to do this work at no extra cost. Although it means losing money on the job, I am more concerned that your clients should be satisfied.

Yours sincerely,

Norriman is in effect saying that he is going to satisfy Rubicon no matter what the cost, although he knows it is not going to be easy. Sadly, there are not an awful lot like him still around, but they usually have full order books.

SUTTON TO TURVY

Dear George, 23.5.70

LABWELS Bench tops

I have been in touch with Norriman of Shefleford Ceramics

and can do no better than enclose a copy of the letter I have just received. As you will see, he seems confident that he can produce a satisfactory finish to the tiles which have been laid. By next week there should be enough completed for us to judge the results. If you like, I will give you a ring around Wednesday and we could have a look at whatever has been finished by then.

Incidentally, I did get Leslie to show me some of the work in Accrington tiles which had been done previously. Whilst I agree it was quite a good standard, it could not by any means be called perfect. I wonder if you have ever examined it in detail? There are tiles which have a slight curvature either one way or the other and there are also places where slight lipping can be detected, although these are not enough to cause any inconvenience in use. I am sure that the reason for the higher standard has nothing to do with the quality of the tiles, but is due to the fact that they were laid on a good thick bed, which gave more opportunity for a skilled tradesman who was picking his tiles carefully to match edge-for-edge and thus lose the discrepancies. Norriman says that if you wish, he will himself demonstrate, using the tiles now on site, how this can be done in those circumstances. I have no doubt that he can.

Yours sincerely,

Sutton seems to have developed a pretty thick skin as far as Turvy is concerned and is not going to be pushed around without complaint. He has long since dropped 'the customer is always right approach' and he is right to do so. Although mindful of where his bread and butter comes from, he also realises he will gain nothing by prostrating himself every time something goes wrong.

The dig at Turvy about previous work might be considered unnecessary, but I think not. People with outrageously biased opinions should not be allowed to get away with it just because they are addressing someone they think is beholden to them. Rubicon are getting at least as much benefit from Sutton's diligent services as he is from their patronage. There seems to have been no reply to this letter (none was really needed) and the next written evidence comes again from Sutton.

SUTTON TO TURVY

Dear George, 30.5.70

LABWELS Bench tiling

This is just to confirm that the finished work by Shefleford which we inspected yesterday was of a satisfactory standard. I must admit I was a bit surprised to see how well it had turned out. Norriman is a bit worried about the time it is taking, but is sticking to his offer to do it at no extra cost, which I think is more than fair. Perhaps when the time for final settlement comes, you might consider a gesture, such as meeting 50% of the extra cost, as a mark of respect for an unexpectedly difficult job well done? The work will take longer than expected, but as it does not prevent other trades, it should not result in any overall extension of time.

Yours sincerely,

Here we have Sutton living up to his role as impartial adjudicator between client and builder. It would have been better, however, to have waited until the whole of the work had been completed and inspected for flaws. To many firms this sort of suggestion would seem like madness, because they work on the principle of never paying more than they have to for anything, however good.

TURVY TO SUTTON

Dear Richard, 1.6.70

LABWELS Tiling

Thank you for your letter. I confirm that what we saw was an acceptable standard of tiling and I hope it can be maintained to the end.

As regards your proposed gesture to Noriman, I do wish I could convince you that we are not running a charity here and that I fail to see why we should pay more than we have to for anything. However, I accept that the tiling under discussion will be of a higher standard than previous work of this type and, therefore, I will consider your suggestion when the time arrives. In the meantime, you can tell Noriman we are pleased with the way the work is going.

Yours sincerely,

SUTTON TO SHEFLEFORD

Dear Mr. Norriman, 2.6.70

Rubicon LABWELS Building

Mr. Turvy of Rubicon has asked me to inform you that he is well satisfied with the standard of finish you are now producing after grinding. When the work is completed, if it remains at this standard, I hope to persuade Rubicon to meet at least part of your extra costs. This is in view of the fact that the standard they are now getting is a better job than they have previously expected using these materials. I expect to be able to have a decision on this at the time we reach virtual completion of the contract.

Yours sincerely,

23

Mrs. Beeton and Her Wiles

MRS. BEETON TO SUTTON

Dear Richard, 16.5.70

I had a look at my new office the other day and I must say it looked a bit small to me, although everyone tells me all rooms look like that before they are decorated or furnished.

I am really writing to say a little bird told me you have a thing in your contract called a PC Sum which is for me to spend decorating and furnishing my office. You know how the top brass in our sort of world are so conservative about these things and rely on using the styles and fashions of yesterday so that they feel safe and credit themselves with impeccable taste. Well, I want something which is right up to date and still in impeccable taste. I'm sure you know the kind of thing I mean. Nothing gaudy; restrained use of colour and pattern; nice use of timber veneers, simply designed carpets and curtains with plenty of texture, but not knee-deep in pile. In other words, I want a room where the atmosphere is so impeccable my visitors notice nothing but a feeling of serenity. Do you think we can manage that? I'm no slouch myself when it comes to interior design, and if you will draw what we need, I will deal with the colours etc.

Could we possibly meet here at 12.00 noon or thereabouts on Wednesday to discuss the matter in more detail?

Yours,

SUTTON TO MRS. BEETON

Dear Dora, 18.5.70

Many thanks for your letter. I get the general idea, but please don't run away with the notion that you have a King's ransome to spend. To say that a PC Sum is 'for you to spend' is not quite the true situation. There are a number of such sums in the contract but they are put there to cover the cost of items which cannot be exactly described at the tender stage. They are, in fact, my estimate of what a normal scale and quality of provision will cost.

At the time I made these estimates I did not personally know you, otherwise I might have doubled the figure! As it is, we are stuck with it and the situation on the rest of the PC and Provisional sums is such that I must look for under-spending rather than an increase, to help me balance out some of the items which have gone up for reasons entirely outside my control. These, however, will not be so recognised by my masters who will be expecting me to break even. It's a hard life!

Sorry, I can't make Wednesday, but will Friday do at the same time?

Yours sincerely,

Sutton went to his meeting on Friday and dictated the following immediately afterwards. Meetings of this sort at which a lot of decisions may be taken are best recorded carefully.

SUTTON TO MRS. BEETON (PERSONAL)

Dear Dora, 24.5.70

LABWELS

I am writing to confirm the points we agreed at our meeting this afternoon. I am not, however, sending copies as this letter is not intended for distribution to all and sundry. It is simply a record of what we have agreed between ourselves.

1. The PC Sum in the Bill of Quantities which is supposed to cover the cost of this work is £650. At the time I thought that it was fairly generous (but of course I had not met you).

2. I produced a layout for the room based on my idea of what you would require, in the light of your comments in the past.

3. You found this would meet your needs very well with a few

"A little bird told me you have a thing called a PC sum . . ."

detailed changes which I will incorporate and submit again for your approval. I do not anticipate any problems there and in fact, when the job is complete, I am sure you will be very pleased.

4. My rough estimate of the cost of these provisions was £1,200. Since returning to my office, I have spoken to James le Mesurier and he confirms my figure.

5. To simply go ahead without telling anyone about it would doubtless bring down my masters' wrath and I feel sure you would not want that. I am, therefore, relying on you to prepare the ground for the time when everything has to be accounted for. There are a few ways of shifting costs sideways, when there is not a clear distinction between one element and another and we will do what we can in that respect.

6. We discussed the question of a private washroom opening off your office, but I must point out that not even senior management have that. What they do have, however, is a management washroom which is not labelled on the outside as such. In the canteen, there is only the staff female lavatory, which is hardly convenient for the male visitors that you sometimes get.

We both agreed, however, that now is not a good time to raise this matter, during what I call a 'hair shirt period' through which the Company seems currently to be passing. What I have already done, in fact, is to arrange the staff lavatories, which are (by design) next to your office, so that the last loo and associated space can easily be separated from the rest and entered by a door from your office. I feel sure you will not be in occupation very long before the need becomes apparent, and the fortunate ease of this small alteration will be discovered.

I think that is all. As soon as I have modified plans available I will submit them for final approval by you, and then get tenders for doing the work. I think it will be best to employ an interior fittings specialist. Have you anyone you wish to be included? If so, let me know now because I want to give the maximum possible warning and we are already tight for time.

Yours sincerely,

MRS. BEETON TO SUTTON

Dear Richard, 25.5.70

Thank you for your letter. You have summarised the content

of our discussion perfectly and there is nothing I wish to add. I have now received the drawings and there are some details I would like to change but nothing to prevent you seeking prices. In that respect, however, I can save you some trouble because I only want you to ask one firm.

For a good many years now we have been using the services of Gerry & Johns for all canteen furniture and the like. They are very good and being regular customers we get very good service. I can also guarantee that the price they will give you will be less than you would get from any of the other firms in the business. I can do this because I shall tell them that they must, and they are very anxious to stay in my good books. Did you know, by the way, that in the trade no one would ever give you a lower price for us because they each respect the territory of their competitors? I can't put it any better than that and some would say it is disgraceful, but we have no complaints as to the standards or the price. They are not cheap, of course, but how often do you get a good job from someone who is?

I have told them to expect your enquiry.

Yours,

SUTTON TO MRS. BEETON

Dear Dora, 26.5.70

You'll get me shot!

I have sent the drawing and details to Gerry & Johns and I will be arranging to see them next week in London to get a general idea of their methods and see some other work they have done. If there are no snags we should be able to get them on site in a month which should be soon enough.

I hope you haven't got any more tricks up your sleeve!

Yours sincerely,

SUTTON TO GERRY & JOHNS

Dear Sirs, 26.5.70

New Canteen Building for Rubicon Ltd.

This building is nearing completion and contains an office for the canteen manageress which is to be equipped and decorated to a standard which reflects the fact that it is the centre of the provision of what might be called social services provided by the company for their own staff and also for guests.

I understand that, over the years, you have done quite a lot of work for this company to their apparent satisfaction. I have never worked with you before although I have seen some of the work you have done for Leverpullers Ltd. where I worked for a number of years.

I now enclose a drawing and a brief specification for the work to be done in the manageress's office, which consists of all the internal finishes (floor, walls and ceiling) fixed fittings and loose furniture. You need not include for connecting services which will be done by the appropriate sub-contractors who will still be on site when you are there.

The drawing is not intended to be a full production drawing, as I believe that joinery details etc. are best left to you, whose trade it is. This being so, I think it would be well if we could meet to discuss details before you submit your price. I would prefer to do this at your office where I imagine I could see examples of your work in progress and perhaps some recently completed jobs? I have other business in London at the end of the month and it would fit in well with my other plans if I could see you on Friday 31st at 2.00 p.m. I do hope this will be convenient.

Yours faithfully,

GERRY & JOHNS TO SUTTON

Dear Sir, 27.5.70

Rubicon Ltd. LABWELS Building

Thank you for your esteemed enquiry re Mrs. Beeton's office at the above. We shall of course be delighted to submit a quotation. We had actually been expecting your enquiry because Mr. H. W. Dowel, our area representative, was told by Mrs. Beeton during his last routine visit to expect it. You will appreciate that we do a lot of business in the supply of moveable furniture in which there is no involvement by an architect, although we are also quite accustomed to the type of work in your present enquiry.

We shall look forward to meeting you at 2.00 p.m. on the 31st and as this is just after normal lunchtime we hope you will be free to lunch with us here. Our senior staff dining room is naturally a bit of a showplace, considering the business we are in. May we suggest 12.30?

Yours faithfully,

GERRY & JOHNS TO SUTTON

Dear Sir, 3.6.70

LABWELS Building

We have pleasure in enclosing our quotation for the work to Mrs. Beeton's office, which as you will see totals £1,157.50. This includes everything on your drawing as discussed at our office, except for the electric light fittings which we understand you will arrange for through the electrical contractor, so that the client gets the benefit of trade discounts unobtainable by us.

As to the quality of the work, it should be roughly equivalent to some of the samples of other work we showed you. That is to say, it will not be a luxury job in the manner of our staff dining room, but it will be properly put together and finished in the tradition of good-class English joinery. We feel sure you will be satisfied with it when completed. If you are not, we undertake to bring it up to the standard you expected.

If we could have your immediate approval we can be on site within a month, which we understand would meet your requirements. Once on the site we expect we could complete in a further month, or at the most, six weeks.

Yours faithfully,

The undertaking in the penultimate paragraph could be rather dangerous in the hands of an unscrupulous architect or client, but no doubt, Gerry & Johns have made their own assessment of Sutton and had it confirmed by Mrs. Beeton. It certainly gives their letter an air of calm confidence which will, and is no doubt intended to, impress.

SUTTON TO KNOTT & BANISTER

Dear Sirs, 4.6.70

LABWELS

I enclose a copy of a quotation received from Gerry & Johns, the interior finishes and furniture specialists. I should be obliged if you will place your order for this work immediately, as we need them on site in approximately one month from now.

The final details have yet to receive the approval of Mrs. Beeton, but any changes will be minor and, if necessary, will be dealt with directly between myself and Gerry & Johns.

Yours faithfully,

SUTTON TO MRS. BEETON

Dear Dora, 4.6.70

I have had Gerry & Johns' quotation which came in at £1,157.50 excluding electric light fittings, so we couldn't have been much closer. I have told Knott & Banister to place their order, although there may still be some minor alterations.

Gerry & Johns also sent a perspective of how the job should look which as usual is slightly glamourised, but gives the general idea. There are one or two things about the detailing of the furniture I am not too happy with, and unless I hear to the contrary, I will call on you when I make my next site visit on Wednesday bringing the perspective with me. I don't want to fold it for posting.

Yours sincerely,

SUTTON TO GERRY & JOHNS

Dear Sirs, 7.6.70

LABWELS Building

You should by now have received the official order for this work from the main contractors, Knott & Banister. Since instructing them I have had a discussion with Mrs. Beeton and there are two things we would like to have changed from the details, as they appear in your perspective view. They are as follows:

1. The conference table to have rounded corners (about 6″ radius) and the supports to be in the form of two trestles leaving the perimeter free of legs which obstruct seating.
2. The desk to have rounded corners to match, and the two consoles below to be free-standing, each with one filing drawer and one shallow drawer.

I hope this will not cause any problems or adversely affect your price, and I would be glad of confirmation to that effect.

Yours faithfully,

It appears that Sutton had his meeting with Mrs. Beeton and that they jointly agreed on these changes. Freedom to make such changes is a necessary part of any bespoke article, but when these involve a change from a maker's standard practice they do involve a risk which G & J are quick to point out.

GERRY & JOHNS TO SUTTON

Dear Sir, 9.6.70

LABWELS Building

We have your letter re changes and are arranging to have these carried out. We must point out, however, that whilst we appreciate the desirability of leaving a free perimeter, it is not our normal practice because of the difficulty of avoiding tilting under the stresses imposed by heavy elbow leaners. The legs, if carefully positioned, do not cause much of an obstruction. Thus, we cannot give you the unconditional guarantee we mentioned on this item.

The other changes present no difficulties.

We should add about £20 for the table, but for the sake of goodwill, this being our first job for you, we will leave the price as it is.

Yours faithfully,

Fair enough! Trestle type tables are notorious for their tendency to tilt.

KNOTT & BANISTER TO SUTTON

Dear Sir, 7.6.70

LABWELS

We have your instruction to order office furnishing etc. from Gerry & Johns. This we have done but we are not happy with them.

We had them on a job for Leverpullers five years ago and they were nothing but trouble. They never appeared on site on the dates agreed and when they did appear they expected everyone else to run around after them, especially electrics and plumbers. They behaved as if we didn't exist (except to off-load for them etc.) and would only take instructions from the architect or the client.

I called them a lot of prima donnas, although in the end they did turn out a decent job. Anyway, it pleased Leverpullers, and that's not easy.

We must warn you, however, that if they start poncing around the place like Nureyev there will be a few choice remarks from our lot who arn't used to that sort of thing.

Yours faithfully,

This doesn't sound like Steele of Knott & Banister and it turns out not to be.

KNOTT & BANISTER TO SUTTON

Dear Mr. Sutton, 9.6.70

LABWELS

We have just seen our last letter to you re Gerry & Johns and hasten to apologise. Our Mr. Steele has taken a week's leave and left Geordie Stokoe, his general foreman, in charge. Geordie is no respecter of persons and suffers from the delusion that he can conduct correspondence as well as the next man, especially if he can get his hands on a shorthand typist.

As he says, he once had the experience of these interior specialists on his site and it made an indelible mark on his soul.

Steele will be back next week and I would be grateful if you could just try to ignore any efforts to supplant him!

Yours sincerely,

This is signed by Banister who shows a well-developed sense of humour. I will never forget the pitying kindness I received when first finding myself the only Sassenach in a detachment of twenty Geordies. They did their best to teach me how to speak 'proper' the way they do north of the Tees, and made it clear that I was not to blame, for not having been born there.

We may hear more of Gerry & Johns later.

DRAUGHTSMAN TO SUTTON (PRIVATE)

Dear Richard, 9.6.70

LABWELS

Although I have heard nothing from you on the subject, it has come to my notice (via Stokoe and Harris) that you have authorised the placing of an order for Mrs. Beeton's office interior for almost £1,200 against a PC Sum of only £650. It may not surprise you to learn that I have heard that spoken of as excessive. Mrs. Beeton is noted for her capacity to twist important people round her little finger and this does not endear her to some not quite so important people.

Harris is not in the least concerned. The more they are paid the more likely they are to do a good job, and the less likely they are to get in his hair. However, it has now come to George Turvy's ears and he is livid. I have had a smart

". . .poncing about the place like Nureyev. . ."

dressing down for not keeping a closer eye on spendthrift you, and I expect he will find some way of making his displeasure felt.

I thought I had better warn you.

Yours sincerely,

MRS. BEETON TO SUTTON (PERSONAL)

Dear Richard, 9.6.70

LABWELS

I hear there is a witchhunt going on about the cost of the finishings in my office, principally from those who think they are entitled to a better standard than I am.

This letter is to put your mind at rest. As you know, we recently got a new Chairman and I took care, as I always do, to find out what there was to know about him. He sounded rather forbidding, but actually he is a sweetie, and when I met him recently we had quite a long chat. He is not really interested in side issues like canteens, but when I put it to him that at least they had a valuable function to perform in relation to the Company's guests, especially in a place like Winterfield, he fully agreed. From there it was a small step to the point that the manageress should have a decent place to welcome guests as well as run the job, and he heartily agreed. I can assure you J.J. is on my side and so is Prop Steadman, so we have nothing to fear. I hear George Turvy is on the warpath, but he will find himself in a minority of one. George has become quite impossible recently. He used to be a nice friendly man, but recently I think he's been under a lot of pressure from the top and it's all got to come out somewhere.

I am looking forward to the arrival of Gerry & Johns after which I will be on site every day!

Yours with thanks for trying hard,

24

Coats of Many Colours

DRAUGHTSMAN TO SUTTON

Dear Richard, 22.5.70

LABWELS

As you know, we are now getting towards completion and a

particularly difficult time is beginning for everyone on site, especially the main contractor. As usual, we have several trades on the site at once. Electricians, heating engineers and plumbers are all engaged on second fix, as are the joiners and ceiling fixers. The lift engineers are now also on site.

It is our intention to lock rooms as they are completed and clean them ready for the painters, but this is not easy. There is dust everywhere and it is hard to keep it out, even with the doors shut. Another problem is the fact there is always some reason why someone must have entry to locked rooms and all and sundry therefore have keys which they pass on to others. No one could ever run a prison this way. I begin to understand what you meant when you said that a building was a far more complex item than a structure. Harris is proving a tower of strength at this stage and I am beginning to see why he is still where he is in spite of his abrasive manner. He seems to know what everybody is doing on each and every day, and somehow keeps them all out of each other's hair.

If we are to meet our completion target we shall have to have the painters in two weeks' time. I think it would be best if they started with the priming of woodwork and then tackled the walls when they have reached undercoat stage.

The external painting can start now and we have arranged for this with Knott & Banister Ltd. next week. The external colour scheme is simple and settled so there is no problem there, but the inside colour selection is still very much up in the air. I wonder if you have had any success in getting agreement on this very touchy subject?

Yours sincerely,

Rubicon is in a rather special situation as it supplies certain machinery and materials to the paint industry. Consequently, Rubicon's management likes to share its own orders out amongst its customers, who otherwise get a bit touchy.

In this case, Sutton has been told to have the order placed with Luxisheen Ltd., who have at Rubicon's request supplied colour schemes for all the interiors. In general, these specify one colour for three walls, another for a so-called feature wall and another for ceilings which are all the same anyway. There are about half a dozen different combinations some of which are used several times over. There are also door, window and accessories colours to go along with the walls. Sutton has left this a bit late. Has he forgotten?

SUTTON TO TURVY

Dear George, 23.5.70

LABWELS

We should have interior painters on the site in two, at the most three, weeks' time if we are to have any chance of meeting our target date. The colour schemes provided by Luxisheen Ltd. are with you, so they could be passed around your colleagues before we all meet to finally settle the matter.

I think the time has come for this to be done. Would you please suggest a suitable date next week (as early as possible) to settle these details? As you know, I am not in favour of this way of doing things which to my mind is just a present-day fad and an understandable reaction against institutional green and cream. Fortunately, it is not difficult to change the colour of paint! In any case I have had a go at a scheme of my own which I hope you will consider alongside Luxisheen's.

Yours sincerely,

This kind of thing seems to have dropped right out of favour today. It was comparatively harmless but gave an importance to paint, that it never should have had. Texture and pattern seemed to have dropped out of fashion.

The meeting must have been arranged by telephone because next we see are the notes which followed it.

NOTES ON A MEETING HELD AT THE OFFICES OF CONDORCO LTD. ON 27.5.70 TO SETTLE THE INTERNAL COLOUR SCHEMES AT LABWELS BY BRUSH & ROLLERMAN LTD.

Present:	H. Steadman	Rubicon Works Manager
	G. Turvy	Rubicon Chief Engineer
	D. Beeton, Mrs.	Rubicon Canteen Manageress
	L. Draughtsman	Rubicon I/c LABWELS Site
	R. J. Sutton	Architect
	H. Higgins	Architect

"Almost a sigh of relief. . ."

1. The colour schemes prepared by Luxisheen Ltd. were tabled. All the Rubicon members had studied these and reactions were varied. Turvy and Steadman thought they would meet the requirements well enough and were 'cheerful'. Mrs. Beeton didn't like that 'kind of thing' and Draughtsman offered no opinion.

2. Sutton gave his views that these kind of schemes were just a passing fashion which would look silly in ten years time, even if they looked superficially attractive now. This met with a cold reception.

3. Sutton tabled his own scheme which was based on the use of almost neutral colours for walls, along with white ceilings and the use of textured materials (e.g. Hessian) to emphasise space enclosure where appropriate. The whole intent would be to provide a background where certain areas could be selected (at the whim of the occupant) for the display of paintings or photographs, probably the latter, to add interest to the environment. He pointed out that for the decoration of public areas the company has quite a lot of material which would be appropriate, some dating back to the early days in Italy.

4. Mrs. Beeton said she liked this idea. She herself had some colourful prints that she had nowhere to display, and which with suitable frames she would be glad to have on exhibition and out of her way at home. This more or less stopped proceedings and for some time there was no comment at all. Eventually, Steadman said that if that kind of thing were to be used, it would be better if the prints were bought or hired and had nothing to do with any particular person who might be regarded as too 'pushy'.

5. Mrs. Beeton accordingly withdrew that suggestion, but put forward the view that, as this building, apart from the Labs. which no one cared about, (Dr. Science was not even at the meeting – had he been asked?) was her responsibility, she should have the final say as to how it should be decorated. This drew unanimous support, almost a sigh of relief, that the whole awkward business could be so easily dealt with.

6. The result was that the meeting gave authority for the architect and Mrs. Beeton, in consultation with Draughtsman, to agree colour schemes and other decorative details, and put the work in hand without need for further consultation.

The painter who said this is the final finish.

SUTTON TO KNOTT & BANISTER LTD.

Dear Sirs, 4.6.70

LABWELS

I have resolved the interior colour scheme with Rubicon and have written to Luxisheen Ltd. with instructions as to what is required. There should be no problems with supplies and it is now up to the painters to confirm their order and get on to the site as soon as you decide it is possible. Rubicon are very sensitive about the standard of painting in their buildings, and I am sure your painting contractors will be aware that a high standard is required.

Yours faithfully,

Unfortunately, they are not. There was nothing in the specification in the Bill of Quantities to warn them that anything special would be required. Of course, specifications always state that the workmanship shall be of the best quality, but this has no meaning unless it is described in specific terms, defining exactly what is to be done at each stage. The price the painters have included does not allow for anything special – why should it?

DRAUGHTSMAN TO SUTTON

Dear Richard, 20.6.70

I would be grateful if you could come and take a look at what the painters say is the final coat on the flush doors. Harris is in no doubt that it will not pass muster and I have already heard rumblings to the effect, 'When are those painters going to put a final coat on something so we can see what sort of a job they are making?' I have not so far had the courage to say, 'That is the final coat,' but we will have to sort it out soon.

Yours sincerely,

SUTTON TO KNOTT & BANISTER

Dear Sirs, 22.6.70

LABWELS

There is some question as to whether your painting sub-contractors, Brush & Rollerman Ltd., are fulfilling the standard set in the specification. So far as I can gather from various people on site, Brush & Rollerman *think* they are doing a normal job as specified, but our clients are not of the same opinion. They have, as you know, a vested interest in the painting business.

My clients would like me to convene a meeting on site with you and your painters when a sample of completed work can be inspected and views expressed. They would prefer Monday next week at 11.00 a.m. and I would be obliged if you will arrange accordingly. For the time being, the subject for discussion is the standard of finish on the doors. We would like you also to be represented, to give us the benefit of your long experience of these matters.

Yours faithfully, cc J. le Mesurier

NOTES ON A SITE MEETING HELD ON THE 26.6.70 TO CONSIDER THE STANDARD OF GLOSS-FINISH PAINTWORK BEING ACHIEVED

Present:	G. Turvy	Rubicon Ltd.
	L. Draughtsman	Rubicon Ltd.
	H. Steadman	Rubicon Ltd.
	A. Steele	Knott & Banister
	P. Thinners	Brush & Rollerman
	R. Harris	Rubicon Site engineer
	P. U. Rethane	Luxisheen Ltd.
	R. Sutton	Architects
	H. Higgins	Architects

1. Several doors were examined and the Rubicon members all expressed disatisfaction. It emerged they were not prepared to accept the job as it stood.
2. Several other doors in existing buildings were examined, and there was no question that they were of a considerably higher standard, in spite of being ready for repainting.
3. Close inspection showed the problem to lie in the very grainy plywood used for the face of the flush doors. Even when more coats of gloss were applied, this wood still gave a dull appearance owing to the contained shadow in the texture of the grain.
4. Mr. Thinners explained that such materials were not suitable as a base for the normal painting spec. of KSP* plus two undercoats and one gloss. There was just not sufficient material to fill the grain. However, that was the spec. he had been

asked to work to when pricing and that was what we were now getting.
5. Mr. Turvy asked if a good job could be produced at extra cost and the answer was, 'Yes'. The doors would have to be sanded down, knife-filled, sanded again, brush-filled, sanded again and then receive two undercoats and two gloss, lightly sanded between each coat. The cost would be approximately double that of the original spec.
6. Messrs. Turvy and Steadman consulted, asked for the approximate cost, which Thinners thought would be about £4.00 per door (including frame and architrave), and then gave their instruction to proceed immediately with the super specification, after approval of a sample which could be ready in a week.
7. Knott & Banister said they thought this might result in a delay on their programme, but they would try to re-allocate areas to the painters to keep them going. Harris also thought this should be possible. cc J. le Mesurier

**Stands for knot, stop, prime (perhaps a little passé today).*

TURVY TO SUTTON

Dear Richard, 4.7.70
LABWELS

I saw the sample door yesterday and it is quite up to standard. I gave orders that the painters were to proceed accordingly.

I cannot for the life of me think why you included such a poor specification in the original documents. The additional cost has proved to be comparatively small and I tried to impress upon you at the beginning of this project that we wanted a good standard of building. The work as it was before my intervention could hardly have been considered fit for a cheap speculative housing estate.

I hope that in the coming weeks, whilst the building is being finished off, we shall not have any more unpleasant surprises of this kind.

Yours sincerely,

Turvy should remember that not long ago he expressed a desire for no more unpleasant surprises about additional costs, and at the estimate stage was anxious to keep this to the minimum. However, Sutton should not have been caught out like this. If he had thought about his painting specification whilst deciding on the supply of flush doors, he would have realised that they were not compatible. There are doors available which at very little extra cost do not need such elaborate preparation. Indeed, there are some doors which are not only cheaper, but which would have given a better finish when painted – as the next letter shows.

SUTTON TO TURVY

Dear George, 6.7.70

LABWELS

Thank you for your letter. I am pleased the sample turned out well and we must now see to it that the rest follow suit.

I can understand your disappointment with the finish which the original specification produced. I too was far from happy, but I don't think the fault lies exclusively with me. You may recall that at the outset we were all very much concerned with keeping costs down, and despite the merits of this, there is no doubt that such an attitude does tend to lead to the specification of what may be called the minimum acceptable standard which allows nothing for special situations.

The doors which I specified are obtainable in what is called an SSSSS finish (Super Synthetic Silicone Satin Surface) which is intended for polishing, but which would have provided a first-class base for paint. You may not remember that at that time I also suggested that hardboard-faced doors, which are actually the cheapest of all, are a good base for a painted finish, but you rejected this on the grounds that they are often derisively referred to as 'cardboard' doors.

At the end of the day, I suppose the episode can be laid literally at my door since I did not match the painting spec. to the type of flush doors provided, or vice versa. However, this has now been put to rights and at no greater cost than would have been incurred if the right specification had been used in the first place.

Yours sincerely,

Sutton seems to be becoming increasingly intolerant of Turvy's criticism. He will have to take care because a full-scale confrontation with the client is something to be avoided at all costs, unless the situation can be seen to be inevitable anyway.

The use of the term 'cardboard' in reference to what can be a very good and durable material is unfair to the compressed paperboard industry, but perhaps they deserve it for choosing a name which all too readily rhymes.

SUTTON TO BRUSH & ROLLERMAN

Dear Sirs, 6.7.70

Rubicon Ltd. LABWELS

Further to my discussion with Mr. Thinners I enclose two copies of the general arrangement drawings on which have been added details of the finish, including the colour, to be applied to all surfaces, with additional notes as to the colours of woodwork and metalwork fittings. Also enclosed are the specifications to be used for the various surfaces. These are as described in the original specification, except for the variations already agreed for a better standard on doors and frames etc.

It is not intended to use the colour scheme supplied, at Rubicon's request, by Luxisheen, although it is, however, desired that their paint should be used throughout. However, if Luxisheen cannot supply any particular item, you are at liberty to obtain it from any of your usual sources. This will automatically apply to certain wall finishes, such as hessian or paper, which they do not manufacture.

If you are in doubt about anything, please consult with Knott & Banister, or directly with me.

Yours faithfully,

COPY to Knott & Banister (incl. drawings)
COPY to L. Draughtsman Esq.
ENC. General arrangement drawings annotated for painting.

SUTTON TO KNOTT & BANISTER LTD.

Dear Sirs, 6.7.70

LABWELS Painting

I enclose a set of drawings which have been marked up with details of the interior finishes and colours, as agreed with Mrs. Beeton of Rubicon, together with a detailed specification for the paintwork and other internal finishes. These have all been sent to your sub-contractor, Brush & Rollerman Ltd., plus copies sent to Mr. Draughtsman for his own use and that of Mr. Harris. I hope you can now get everyone going at their best possible speed. When a job gets this near to completion everyone gets restless.

At the risk of sounding repetitive, I would again remind you that Rubicon sets great store by the standard of painting, and I am looking to you to give that extra bit of supervision, that can make all the difference to the finished job.

Yours faithfully,

It may seem strange to see Sutton referring to 'supervision' by Knott & Banister. They are the builders are they not? The answer is, 'Yes', but Brush & Rollerman are the builder's own sub-contractors, selected and appointed by themselves, as opposed to nominated sub-contractors, selected by the architect and appointed by the contractor on the instructions of the architect. This implies that he does not entirely take responsibility for their work, whereas work done by the builder's own sub-contractors is treated exactly the way it would be, as if carried out by his own direct employees. Thus he has a duty to see to it that their work is properly done. There are those who would argue that this also applies to nominated sub-contractors, but I have yet to see it proved on site.

Sutton should not really be corresponding direct with Brush & Rollerman. But K & B are unlikely to make an issue out of that.

There is a school of thought which believes that all sub-contracts should be arranged by the main contractor who would thus have complete control of the site and that all the architects' contact with the job should be channeled through him. It would certainly make life much simpler for the architect once the contract had been let, but it would enormously extend the design and preparation period.

SUTTON TO DRAUGHTSMAN

Dear Leslie,
LABWELS

I enclose a copy of my letters to Brush & Rollerman and to Knott & Banister together with the drawing etc. As you will see, I have again tried to impress on K & B the stress that Rubicon place on painting.

I think this is an occasion on which Harris could be a big help. I am sure he knows the painting trade like the back of his hand, and if he takes a firm stand at the outset, as he so often does, he could easily keep them on the straight and narrow. May I leave it with you?

Yours sincerely,

KNOTT & BANISTER TO SUTTON

Dear Sir, 7.7.70

LABWELS Painting

Our painters Brush & Rollerman have put a point to us about the way this contract has been run. As you know, they are our own appointees, and it was their rates that went into the tender bill. These rates were based on the usual arrangement that they would get their materials from their usual suppliers. It seems these people are Factors who do not deal with Luxisheen, which means that B & R have to go elsewhere. In this case, they have had to go direct to Luxisheen, who do not supply through Factors and the upshot is that this is costing them more than for an equal quality from their usual source.

We know there is a clause in the contract which states that all trade discounts go to the employer (at least on paper) but this is not a question of discounts. It is just that the actual total price they are having to pay is about $7\frac{1}{2}\%$ more than the figure they allowed for when they prepared their tender, and they do not think this fair.

We have to say that we agree with them and that we will be obliged to make a claim on their behalf. It would have been different if Luxisheen had been specified in the bill, but they were not. The extra amount involved is not a lot and we hope the client will see the validity of this claim.

Yours faithfully,

We must hope so too because it is perfectly valid. The next question is to discover why was Luxisheen not specified in the Bills of Quantities. As there is nothing on record to prove it, Sutton has to rely on his memory.

SUTTON TO DRAUGHTSMAN

Dear Leslie,

LABWELS

I fear another of those awkward little things has cropped up which I feel I should report to you. I enclose a copy of a letter which I have received from Knott & Banister, which I trust will be self-explanatory.

There is no question in my mind that they have a justifiable claim which will have to be met. The question which then arises is why Luxisheen was not specified in the Bill. There is nothing on record that I can find, but my memory is quite clear on the matter. When the Bill was being prepared I asked for guidance on the paint, but at that stage no-one had given it a thought and it was pushed aside until later – a by no means unusual occurrence. It is a pity that Luxisheen do not deal with Brush & Rollerman's suppliers but there is quite a lot of the so-called 'closed-shop system' in the paint trade, and I believe it can be quite cut-throat.

My feeling is that having reported this to you, it is one of those things which need go no further, being just a run-of-the-mill variation.

Yours sincerely,

The subject may have been further discussed between Sutton and Draughtsman, but there is nothing on file to Rubicon except the following letter.

SUTTON TO KNOTT & BANISTER

Dear Sirs, 12.7.70

LABWELS

I have cleared the question of extra cost of material to your painters, Brush & Rollerman, with Rubicon (Mr. Draughtsman) and we are agreed that the claim is justifiable. Will you please inform them accordingly.

Yours faithfully, cc J. le Mesurier

Another notable feature of this batch of correspondence is the fact that copies of all the letters concerning the paintwork have been sent to James le Mesurier of Cutt & Shuffle. All matters affecting costs should automatically be reported to the QS. He would most likely have picked it up anyway from the builder's and sub-contractor's invoices which are open to him whenever any question of extras arises.

For some reason, the variations which occur on contracts these days are so extensive that the usual routine of the QS preparing a bill of extra and omissions has almost been abandoned and a complete remeasurement of all items is usually prepared. This means that, in effect, the original

Bill is no more than a means of obtaining tenders and checking costs during progress. The final Bill occasionally takes a long time to prepare, and strangely its is the builder, not the employer, who never seems to be in a hurry.

This is the last we hear about this subject.

25

One for All and All for One

WILLIAM BANISTER TO SUTTON (PERSONAL)

Dar Mr. Sutton,

LABWELS

Mr. Steele sought my opinion on a certain situation which seems likely to develop on site, and I can see he has cause for concern. I am not sure if the matter has yet been drawn to your attention, but it concerns the cork-tile flooring where it is laid on top of asphalt at ground-floor level. Recently, some cracks have developed in rather a random way: it is not possible to detect any sort of pattern, or to relate them to any structural feature – they are just cracks, not very large but spreading.

We have had a look and thought we should investigate further. I got Toughgrain's man up and we cut out a small area of tile. Beneath that was the asphalt which was also cracked in much the same way. After that we had Tarrag's man as well and cut out some of the asphalt. Unfortunately, as you may have guessed, the screed was cracked. The site concrete below seemed sound enough, but even that after thorough cleaning and washing showed signs of hairline shrinkage cracks and the bond between this surface and the underside of the screed was poor.

We would like to meet you on site to discuss this problem and it might be as well also to have that German chap from BCP, who supplied the additives at the same time, because it doesn't seem as though they did much good. The floors cannot be left as they are and will have to be lifted and replaced where necessary. There is not a lot of area involved, but the job will be a pig because of the number of different firms who will be involved.

"He himself had never had any faith in these 'fancy chemical things'. . ."

I am writing to you myself because I can see unpleasant problems looming for all of us when it comes to trying to allocate responsibility for the cost of these remedial works. I look forward to discussing this with you as soon as we have had our site meeting.

Yours sincerely,

LABWELS: NOTES ON A MEETING WHICH TOOK PLACE ON SITE ON 4.7.70 TO CONSIDER THE SITUATION WHICH ARISES AS A RESULT OF THE CRACKS WHICH HAVE APPEARED IN THE CORK-TILE FLOORS

Present:	W. Banister	Knott & Banister
	A. Steele	Knott & Banister
	W. Bunter	Browning & Skim
	S. Limmer	Blackpool Rock Asphalt Co.
	L. Draughtsman	Rubicon Ltd.
	R. Harris	Rubicon Ltd.
	R. J. Sutton	Architects
	H. Higgins	Architects
	E. P. Resin	Toughgrain Floors

A section of the floor had been cut out as described in Mr. Banister's letter. This was examined and the following opinions were expressed.

1. Mr. Resin was adamant that no blame could be placed on Toughgrain Floors since the cork had clearly cracked only because the asphalt below had cracked. Mr. Steele and Mr. Harris pointed out that there were a few cracks in other areas where there was no asphalt.

2. Mr. Limmer likewise pointed out that it could not be blamed on the asphalt because the screed below had cracked. Messrs. Steele and Harris pointed out again that there had been some hairline cracks where there had been no cracks in the screed.

3. Mr. Bunter pointed out that their work had been done strictly in accordance with the instructions from BCP Ltd. who supplied the additives 'Bondtite and Nilshrink'. He said he himself had never had any faith in these 'fancy chemical things'.

4. Mr. Steele said that no one seemed anxious to go one step further and blame the concrete sub-floor, but he thought it

best at this stage to say that after washing down, it had been possible to detect hairline cracks in the concrete surface. These, however, were just the result of floating and were probably there before the screed was laid.

5. The architects drew attention to the absence of anyone from BCP Ltd Mr. Nichtschwinden, their technical expert, should have been there, but had a previous engagement. It had been arranged that he should receive a copy of the notes on the meeting and would make himself available for any future discussions or other events concerning the current problem. It had also been arranged that a sample of the screed where cut out should be sent to him for laboratory testing.

6. Mr. Sutton said that in addition to the various degrees of responsibility already mentioned, he as the architect must be involved as having written the specification in the first place. In this respect he was identified with his client, the employer, as their representative.

He also pointed out that all building inevitably involved the reliance of one trade upon the work of another, and that in this way the trades were mutually responsible for the final result. He hoped, therefore, that a degree of flexibility would replace the rigid attitudes taken at this meeting.

7. The meeting closed with an agreement for each party to consult with their firms and report in one week to the architects the position to be adopted by each firm.

8. After the meeting Draughtsman and Harris had a word with Sutton about the fact that he had 'identified with his client'. In their view, Rubicon as represented by Turvy and Steadman, would not see it that way. They would probably rather see the architect in a commercial light as just one more firm sharing responsibility with the others.

This question has appeared before. The professional, as distinct from the commercial approach, is one whereby the architect is seen as an employee of the client who takes full responsibility for him, as he would for one of his own employees. The other approach, which seems now to have been accepted as normal, is to regard the architect as a separate entity, jointly responsible for all his actions in conjunction with all the firms engaged in the work. This is a pity, because it ignores the architect's special situation as designer and controller of the job and safe-

guarder of the client's interests in all situations, and ultimately may well work against the employer's interests.

As Sutton pointed out at the meeting, the situation where several trades may depend on the actions of others is endemic in the building industry. This is just an extreme case of a normal situation, and it seems to be often Sutton's misfortune to come up against such extremes.

TURVY TO SUTTON

Dear Richard, 5·7·70

LABWELS

It has come to my notice, via Draughtsman, that there is a problem with cork-floor tiles cracking, and that you have had a meeting on site with the firms who may, or may not, be responsible. That is as it should be and I expect you will be able to sort it out and get things put right.

Leslie also told me that in summarising the situation at this meeting, you referred to yourself as our representative, indicating that your involvement was, in effect, the same as ours. I am afraid I cannot take this view and neither can Prop Steadman with whom I discussed it. As you know, we have been happy with what you have done for us so far, but that does not mean we see you as one of our own employees. If we did, I doubt if we would be paying you as much as your present fees. In other words, we see you as anticipating a profit from this job, in much the same way as the contractors who are involved, and we expect you, therefore, to bear the same degree of responsibility.

My last word on this is that out of the various contributors to the failure which has occurred, there is only one firm that can be said, without any possible argument, to have no responsibility, and that is us, the client. We therefore do not expect to take any share of the extra cost, either directly or through some concealed loophole.

Yours sincerely,

So Turvy has laid it on the line. 'It's not our fault and so we do not pay'. If Sutton had, in fact, played the role assigned to him by Turvy, Rubicon would have found themselves a lot worse off than they are at this stage. They want the service, but are not prepared to back up the professionalism that this requires. It is frequently difficult for people steeped in commercialism to see any other point of view.

Turvy's last paragraph sounds ominous. In saying this is his last word, he seems to be ruling out any possibility of further discussion on the subject. Apparently Sutton has taken this to be so, because his usual reaction to such a situation would be to launch into a long discourse on the merits of the professional/client relationship. In this case he says nothing, the wisest course.

The reference to 'some concealed loophole' at the end of the letter adds a rather unpleasant note. It suggests that at some time in the past, Turvy has discovered costs arising from malpractice being sneaked in somewhere else. This dishonesty does happen, but stands little chance of succeeding, providing nobody in the costing process is bent.

NICHTSCHWINDEN TO SUTTON

Dear Sir, 12.7.70

Rubicon Ltd. LABWELS Building

I am sorry I was unable to attend your site meeting of the 4th July owing to a previous appointment.

I have now received from Knott & Banister a sample, cut from the floor of the building. As I think I told you, we have some excellent laboratories but, unfortunately, they are in Germany and so the tests have taken more time than you would wish. I now have them and have pleasure in enclosing a copy for you. Essentially the reports say that enough 'Bondite' and 'Nilshrink' were put in *but*, very unfortunately, too much water was put in for the Nilshrink.

The effect of the 'Nilshrink' is to make the mix sufficiently plastic to apply even when a lot less water is used. As everyone knows using less water makes a stronger screed and one which will not shrink as much. If the usual amount of water is used the 'Nilshrink' mix will be sloppy which leads to excessive floats which brings the cement to the top and leaves less at the bottom where it must be bond. This will mean that the screed when it sets will be worse than it would if nothing at all had been used.

Although our materials are not technically at fault, I should say this situation is very sad for us as for you. My Direktor states we cannot accept any remedial costs but we would be very

happy to supervise repairs without making any charge.
Yours faithfully,

A good solid Teutonic approach. The Germans seem to lead in the field of concrete admixtures, possibly because of the vast quantities used building autobahns and bomb-proof shelters before and during the Second World War. This all seems irrefutable and must surely allow BCP Ltd. to bow out without a stain on their character.

The really intriguing thing about all this is to see how Sutton, through his determination to take no chances with the screeds, has actually created the conditions which led to their failure (with the assistance of the screeder plasterers, of course, which also got past the eagle eye of Higgins).

Sutton, showing more cunning than he would have done a year ago, decides to keep this information to himself and warns Higgins, who has also seen it, to do likewise.

SUTTON TO WILLIAM BANISTER (PERSONAL)

Dear Mr. Banister, 13.7.70
LABWELS

I was conscious of your helpful attitude in writing to me personally when this business of the cracked flooring first came up. Since then, I have received pretty conclusive evidence that the fault lies with your plastering sub-contractors, Browning & Skim. I think their foreman, Bunter, must have had an off day or two. If you remember, he sanctioned the use of Calor-gas heaters when I had specifically excluded anything of the sort and it now seems that he allowed his screeding party to mix using Nilshrink, but with the same quantity of water as for a normal mix. This was disastrous and I cannot think why we have not had far more trouble. I can only think that after the first day or so he realised what he had done and got it right from then on.

I enclose a copy of the BCP laboratory report, which I found fascinating. I do not think we can discount the evidence it presents and I would be interested to know your reaction to it.

So far, BCP's letter and report have been seen by no-one but you and I. As you know, I have my own views on the sharing of liability, in the interests of goodwill and getting the job done. From the evidence we now have, it could be suggested that the cost of the whole work involved in putting this matter to rights should be borne by Browning & Skim. In my view, it would be fairer, and no doubt cheaper overall, if each trade dealt with its own defects, whatever the origin. I think they will accept this proposal and assuming that I have your approval, I mean to write to them on these lines.

I take it you will inform Browning & Skim and arrange for them to do their share of the work, using Nilshrink properly.

Yours sincerely,

SUTTON TO TOUGHGRAIN FLOORS & ALSO TO THE BLACKPOOL ROCK ASPHALT CO.

Dear Sirs, 13.7.70

LABWELS

Following the site meeting on 4th July, I trust your representative reported the proceedings and that you have since had time to consider your attitude to this somewhat complex situation.

The position is, or was, that each trade involved in the total construction of this floor and finishes claims non-responsibility, on the grounds that its product failed because of defects in others. I am in the same position, because the Specification which I produced was, I believe, the right one for the job.

Obviously, if the situation is to be remedied, some degree of flexibility is needed. I have discussed this matter with the main contractors and we are agreed that the easiest and most equitable way to deal with the problem is to forget the responsibility of other trades and for each to undertake to put right his own work, starting of course with the screeders.

Although there is not a lot of remedial work involved, the matter could drag on for ages unless this reasonable course of action is taken. Clearly, the defects have to be dealt with before occupation, and we do not want to have an unsettled wrangle going on into the maintenance period and beyond.

I would be pleased to hear that you are in agreement.

Yours faithfully,

c/c Knott & Banister

TOUGHGRAIN FLOORS TO SUTTON

Dear Sir, 15.7.70

LABWELS

We acknowledge your letter and agree with what you say. We will repair our own work at our own cost. We are contacting Knott & Banister re details.

Yours faithfully,

BLACKPOOL ROCK ASPHALT CO. TO SUTTON

Dear Sir, 16.7.70

LABWELS

We have your letter about sharing the responsibility for the failure of the cork floors in certain places. We are afraid we cannot agree to this. Superficially it seems fair, but it so happens we were curious enough to contact BPC Ltd., to find out why the screed cracked. They informed us that it was due to the wrong mix being used. This being so, it seems to us that the blame lies fairly and squarely on the shoulders of the plasterers who laid it, and we see no reason why we should be asked to pay for the mistakes of other trades.

We must assume that at the time of your letter you were unaware of this situation and that you will now issue revised directions.

Yours faithfully,

Sooty's philanthropy has backfired. People like to be consulted if they are being asked to contribute, and whatever his theories about the right and wrongs of running a contract, he shouldn't let people in for things without asking them first.

SUTTON TO WILLIAM BANISTER (PERSONAL)

Dear Mr. Banister, 17.7.70

LABWELS Floor defects

I have a rather embarrassing situation on the above which puts a spoke in the wheel of the arrangement I had agreed with you. I enclose a copy of a letter from the BRA Co. who, to my surprise, have been in touch themselves with BCP Ltd. I suppose I should have foreseen something of the sort and consulted them first. As you can see, they are giving me the benefit of the doubt as to whether or not I knew the real situation when I wrote to them.

Without getting involved in formal correspondence etc., I wonder whether you could have a word on the 'phone with them and see if they could still be persuaded to go along with the rest, for the sake of peace and harmony? I think they might respond to that and you can blame it all on me if you like.

Yours sincerely,

WILLIAM BANISTER TO SUTTON (PERSONAL)

Dear Mr. Sutton, 20.7.70

LABWELS

A brief note to let you know that I have now spoken to Stan Limmer of the BRA Co. He eventually saw some merit in the idea, but the trouble is that in our business so many people have been screwed right down to the very letter of a contract at some time or other, that it leaves a permanent mark on them. Limmer is a decent enough man, but he wanted some sop to his dignity so I offered to pay any travelling expenses and he jumped at it. You can now treat the matter as closed.

Yours sincerely,

William Banister is a good man to have on your side. Sooty takes him at his word and replies to the letter from Turvy which he, wisely, had decided to ignore for the time being.

SUTTON TO TURVY

Dear George, 22.7.70

LABWELS

I am writing in response to the letter I had from you a few weeks ago on the subject of defects in the cork-tile floors which involved other trades who had been employed in providing the sub-floors beneath them. This was a complicated situation in which I, as the specifier, was also involved. You will remember that you disagreed with my interpretation of the professional situation, in which as your architect, I found myself.

I am happy to report that after discussion and negotiation with the several parties involved, they have all accepted a compromise solution under which they each accept responsibility for the repair of defects in their own work at their own expense, but without any claim on the other trades involved. This means, of course, that the work will be rectified without any cost to Rubicon.

In reaching this settlement I would like to acknowledge the value of the assistance given by Knott & Banister. I would also like to reassure you that as the faulty method of working was realised at an early stage, the defects in this comparatively small area will almost certainly not be repeated elsewhere.

Yours sincerely,

TURVY TO SUTTON

Dear Sooty, 24.7.70

LABWELS

Thank you for your letter concerning the troubles with the cork-tile floors. Naturally, I am relieved a satisfactory solution has been found and I would be grateful if you could also convey my appreciation to Knott & Banister of the assistance you had from them.

I hope it should not be too long now before we are able to occupy the new building. Our Chairman would like to have an official opening ceremony and I shall be looking to you to organise the 'golden key' side of affairs. I will tell Leslie Draughtsman that he had better start talking to you about it.

Yours sincerely,

26

Trouble with the Lift

KNOTT & BANISTER TO SUTTON

Dear Sir, 28.6.70

LABWELS Lift installation

Messrs. Lockersley Lifts Ltd. have been on the site for about two weeks now. This was none too soon as we ifnormed them that the shaft etc. was ready at least a month ago. Even now they are on the site, it seems clear to us they are not going to complete on time if they go on the way they are at the moment.

We are not holding them up, although they may possibly make this excuse to you. All the bases and fixings, foundation sockets etc. shown on their drawings are completed. We have had these people before and can say they are experts at procrastination.

We believe Lockersley have the staff to finish on time if they can be convinced to give this job the priority it needs. It occurs to us that you or your clients may have some influence that can be usefully brought to bear.

Yours faithfully,

This is true. The appointment of lift sub-contractors is almost always in the hands of the architect and his clients, who often have very strong personal preferences. These were probably acquired as the result of spending innumerable nights in multi-storey hotels, or days in multi-storey offices, where the quality of life is largely controlled by the quality of the lift installation.

In this case, Sutton has made rather a grave error. He has appointed a lift contractor on the basis of four competitive tenders without consulting his client. This is hard to believe, but he may have raised the question at a time when everyone was busy with what seemed then to be more important things.

Now Sutton has a problem. He himself knew nothing of the track record of Lockersley Lifts when he appointed them, since he has not had them on one of his jobs before. The fact that the lifts are manufactured not far from Winterfield predisposed him towards them (although it should not have done) and he once made a visit to their works on an RIBA Branch outing, on which occasion Lockersley provided beer and sandwiches. This, however, was unlikely to be enough to corrupt any of the members. Sutton knows well that Lockersley are not the 'Rolls Royce' of lift installers, but then he has assumed that Rubicon would not be prepared for such extravagance. He feels a bit uneasy at not having gone into detail with Turvy before this, and now decides to use the progress query as an opportunity to open discussions.

SUTTON TO TURVY

Dear George, 30.6.70

LABWELS Lift

Leslie Draughtsman has suggested I approach you direct on this subject because it is a matter which should really have been gone into at upper management level when other design decisions were being taken, but appears to have been pushed aside. Rightly or wrongly, I got the impression that as far as Rubicon were concerned, a lift was a lift just as long as it went up and down and did not break down too often. As a result, I obtained four prices and used the lowest submitted by Lockersley Lifts Ltd., who as you know are a local firm. Although they do not have a reputation for super-de-luxe installations, as far as I am aware, there is nothing to suggest that they have a bad break-down record.

The point in writing now on this subject is that I have had a complaint from Knott & Banister. Apparently, Lockersley were late getting on to the site and they are going to be even later finishing, unless someone can put a bomb under them. K & B admit they have no pull as they haven't had Lockersley before, and as I have never used them previously, I cannot apply much leverage either.

As Lockersley is a local company, it occurred to me you might have some contacts who could bring some influence to bear. If you can exert any pressure I would be grateful. Apart from that, the only thing to be said is that non-operation of the lift when the building opens would not be a disaster, since it can operate without it. Nevertheless, it would be an inconvenience which I would like to avoid if at all possible.

Yours sincerely,

TURVY TO SUTTON

Dear Richard, 2.7.70

LABWELS Lift

Thank you for your letter. Certainly you have been dilatory about informing us of your choice of lift manufacturer, but I suppose we are partly to blame for not having stressed our preferences earlier. As you say, there seemed to be more pressing things to deal with at the time, but I would have liked to have gone into the matter with you because some of my colleagues are very sensitive about lifts and have firmly rooted prejudices. I fear that when they are told we have Lockersley on the job, there are going to be loud groans. The fact they are behind time is a situation for which I believe they hold some kind of record. If asked, we would have suggested including the firm of Too-Good Miss Ltd., whose reputation and prices are high. At least we could have had a chance to decide if it was worth it.

However, that seems to be all water under the bridge. The answer to your query is therefore that we are quite likely to be able to twist Lockersley's tail from more than one direction and I will see what can be done. In the meantime, I think it would be astute to tell K & B that they can make known the threat of action from this direction – possibly it might have some immediate effect if it reaches the right ears. I think we will get our lift on time even though we might not like it.

Yours sincerely,

Turvy could certainly not have been blamed for rapping Sutton's knuckles rather smartly for going ahead on something as delicate as a lift installation with getting it agreed on all sides. I fear we may not of heard the last of that. Apparently Turvy's contacts were effective because next we see:

KNOTT & BANISTER TO SUTTON

Dear Sir, 5.7.70

LABWELS Lifts

This letter is to let you know that whatever action you were able to take with regard to the slow progress being made by Lockersley Lifts Ltd. has certainly been effective. Their work-orce has been doubled, which is all the job can stand, and it now looks as though they have a good chance of completing before the opening date.

The other finishing trades are maintaining progress and we hope shortly to be able to give you a date on which we can clear the building (apart from minor odds and ends) to let the cleaners move in.

Yours faithfully,

DRAUGHTSMAN TO SUTTON

Dear Richard,

LABWELS

Today I took our Managing Director, J. J. Boffin round the job on his first proper conducted tour. Harry (Prop) Steadman was with him and Prop has a keen eye for a straight line and a true plane so it was no casual tour. Things in general seemed reasonably satisfactory and I got the impression that the work was at least as good as had been expected. Naturally, they were both delighted to find a few pigs ears which must be put right.

Just as we were leaving, we found the lift engineers were testing out so we were able to sample its operation. Unfortunately, I am sorry to say that J.J. did not like it and I thought for one awful moment that he was going to order Lockersley's men to rip it out immediately.

I wonder if you realise what a primitive thing it is? It has the old-fashioned multi-leaf gates to car and landing, both of which have to be manually operated and feel as heavy as lead. The speed would offend any self-respecting snail. I know it is only one storey, but I'm afraid even that seems to take about half a minute, plus the fact it is noisy and jerky.

I apologise if you think I am pitching it rather strongly, but I wanted you to be fully aware of the impression that has been created. For all I know you may already have had this from others. I intended to put George Turvy in the picture, but he was away for the day. I will let him know tomorrow.

Sorry to be the bringer of bad news.

Yours sincerely,

This situation shows up Sutton's lack of experience. It is quite possible that Sutton approached the design of this building without ever having had to make an important decision on a lift installation. Although there have doubtless been lifts in buildings he has previously designed, it is quite likely that when this occurred (say at Leverpullers) the decisions regarding the lifts were taken by others, and all he was called upon for was the provision of the shaft etc. Had he ever had to deal with all the technicalities of lift installations, he would not have fallen into this trap. This shows that a qualified architect with getting on for ten years post-graduate experience (and two pre-graduate) is still without detailed knowledge of an essential part of many buildings. Some, perhaps most, architects may go to their grave, (or retirement, whichever comes first) with no knowledge of some of the more esoteric aspects of their profession.

RECORD OF TELEPHONE MESSAGE
FROM TURVY TO SUTTON ON 2.8.70

Subject: LABWELS Lift Installation

George Turvy said he had been briefed about the present

situation by Leslie Draughtsman who showed him a copy of the letter to me. Turvy said he had not realised how bad the lift situation was and that an early meeting must be arranged to discuss it. I explained that as I had envisaged the type of traffic using the lift gave it the general aspect of a goods lift, I had planned accordingly. He said, it would, however, be partly in use as a passenger lift and somehow or other we must look at ways to alter it to suit this use. I said I was not very hopeful about that, but given a day or two would investigate. I concluded the conversation by saying I would then report to the meeting.

SUTTON TO LOCKERSLEY LIFTS LTD.

Dear Sirs, 5.8.70

Lift Installation at Rubicon

Following the visit of your Mr. Pitwell to this office, I am writing to confirm that you are to look into the possibility of modifying the cab and doors on the installation you are just completing to make them automatic. There is to be a meeting at Rubicon's offices on August 8th to discuss this subject and it would help me considerably if you could by then establish the feasibility of this alteration, and have Mr. Pitwell standing by to speak to the meeting if necessary. It would be best if he were to come to my office first and we could then proceed together. I will let you have exact details tomorrow.

Yours faithfully,

RECORD OF A MEETING AT THE OFFICES OF RUBICON ON 8.8.70 TO DECIDE ON WHAT ACTION, IF ANY, SHOULD BE TAKEN TO IMPROVE THE LOCKERSLEY LIFT INSTALLATION

Present:	J. J. Boffin	M. D. Rubicon Ltd.
	Dr. D. Science	Research Director
	G. Turvy	Chief Engineer
	L. Draughtsman	I/c project for Rubicon
	H. Steadman	Works Manager
	R. J. Sutton	Architect

Mr. F. Pitwell of Lockersleys was available for consultation, but not present during the whole meeting.

1. Mr. Turvy took the chair, but it was agreed that no formal minutes would be taken. He outlined the position to the effect that the existing lift is a minor disaster and can only be tolerated if there is no other course than to replace it completely. There were no dissenters from this point of view.
2. The meeting in general then aired its views about the lack of communication which had allowed such stupidity to be translated into fact. It was made clear that both Turvy and I were under fire.
3. I made the point that I had regarded the installation as a goods lift with only occasional passenger use, bringing in the point that the building is only two-storey and most people will use the stairs. G.T. associated himself with this position.
4. Prop Steadman drew attention to the fact that the building was designed for a third storey should the need ever arise.
5. Having allowed time for a full airing of recriminations, I reported that my discussions with Lockersley indicated that means were available whereby the lift could be converted to automatic door operation. I then suggested that Mr. Pitwell be called to speak.
6. Mr. Pitwell said that Lockersley's design department had looked into the matter, and that auto-action could be fitted. This would involve removing and altering the car, thereby slightly reducing its size to leave space in the shaft for the operating gear. The cost of this had not been worked out in detail, but would be in the region of £1,200. It was too late to finish the job before the opening day, and as the work was now complete and the lift operational, it would be best to leave this alteration to be dealt with after occupation.
7. Mr. Steadman asked, as a point of interest, what would have been the cost of automatic operation if it had been included in the first place. Mr. Pitwell could not be certain but thought about half as much. The meeting was left to draw its own separate conclusions and no further comments were made.
8. It was agreed that Lockersley be instructed to proceed with the modifications as soon as possible after the building came into use. Mr. Pitwell then left.
9. There followed some general discussion and someone commented that during his tour of inspection the Chairman, Sir Sidney Rough, should be carefully steered clear of the lift. It emerged that large companies are very sensitive about being

thought 'old-fashioned' and that Chairmen find it a particularly delicate matter.

10. There was no further business. I agreed with Leslie D. to try and pin Lockersley down to some dates for the work on site.

Looking back, Sutton must have been very worried about this episode. It is the sort of thing which often can lead to disillusionment and intolerance on the part of the client, with the result they do not employ an architect again.

This time the situation was not irredeemable, and no-one appears to have suggested that Sutton pay the difference between the £600 and £1,200 it is going to cost to put it right. Perhaps this is because Turvy is also involved and they could hardly stop it out of his salary. In any case, there is still a long way to go before the final account is settled and the job can be 'put to bed'.

27

The Discount Business

WILLIAM BANISTER TO SUTTON (PERSONAL)

Dear Mr. Sutton,

LABWELS

I am again taking the somewhat unusual step of writing personally to you concerning a matter which I fear might lead to a delicate situation. It concerns discount on the Gerry & Johns work.

As you know, under the RIBA form of Contract the only discounts which we, the general contractors, are allowed to keep are the normal monthly cash discount for prompt payment. Any trade discounts, allowed in accordance with normal trade procedures, are to be credited to the benefit of the employer. If we wish to take anything further on these purchases we must include it in our priced bill at the time of the tender.

There are some exceptions to this rule which you as the architect are not supposed to know about, and which come about because of the insistence of some trade organisations on reserving certain discounts to their own members, and not allowing them to anyone else.

This case is similar in principle, but not the same. It seems that in this context Rubicon Ltd. were regarded as non-trade customers, but G & J slipped them the extra 5% through some sort of back door. The straight trade discount of 7½% was allowed in the normal way. We apparently are regarded as 'Trade' and therefore entitled to the extra 5%, but this must not be passed on to our customers. They are now asking us how it is to be paid, and have indicated, verbally only, that they expect it should go to the same back door, i.e. that they expect Rubicon will want it, even though strictly speaking they are not entitled to it.

As I said at first, I thought I should let you deal with this, as there seems to be the making of a nice little scandal if not carefully handled.

Yours sincerely,

There does indeed. What should Sooty do? The easiest and probably safest way would be to leave well alone and let Gerry & Johns pay it in their usual way. That wouldn't do for Sooty, however. It is far too simple and if there is a slight smell of graft anywhere he will pounce on it. He decides on a cautious approach.

SUTTON TO MRS. BEETON (PERSONAL)

Dear Dora, 17.7.70

LABWELS. Gerry & Johns

I have had a letter from Mr. Banister of Knott & Banister about some question of a special discount from Gerry & Johns payable only to the trade, (i.e. the furnishing industry and its suppliers). Apparently, in the present situation at least, K & B Ltd. are regarded as trade. They receive the normal discount of 7½% which under the contract goes to Rubicon. This should be the case with any other discounts, but their Association does not permit this and the extra 5% can not be passed on. If it were, it would be dis-allowed.

Where I need your advice is that it seems that as good customers, although not strictly trade, you do get the 5%, but it is paid into a separate account. G & J are asking where it should be paid this time. K & B Ltd. would not be bothered where it went, since they did not expect such a discount in the first place.

I would be very grateful for your advice.

Yours sincerely,

As might be expected, this caused a rustling in the dovecotes with no-one very anxious to put pen to paper, apart from a hasty note from Dora Beeton.

MRS. BEETON TO SUTTON (PERSONAL)

Dear Mr. Sutton, 18.7.70
LABWELS Canteen Office

Thank you for your letter. I think you must realise this is a fairly confidential matter and I feel it would be best if we met to discuss it.

Yours,

RECORD OF MEETING WITH MRS. BEETON IN THIS OFFICE ON 22.7.70 (STRICTLY CONFIDENTIAL)

Subject: Additional discount payments made by Gerry & Johns.
Present: D. Beeton and R. J. Sutton only.

Mrs. Beeton said that she wanted me to understand the situation quite clearly because what might look, at first sight, very suspect behaviour, was in fact only a slightly unorthodox (sic) way of doing good.

It seems that G & J's extra 5% has always been paid into a separate account, which is not connected with Rubicon directly and does not appear in their books. G & J are not the only source of income either. Its existence is known to only a few people, but these do include some top management. It is used for what Mrs. Beeton describes as charitable ends, although she admits that in this case charity sometimes 'begins at home'.

Its books are audited and there is no need for me to know any more about it, indeed it is better that I should not.

As Knott & Banister have become involved it is better in this case that they should follow the accepted procedure and keep the 5% for themselves. They are hardly likely to object to this. RECORD ENDS.

It is often strange what you may find when you turn over a stone that has been there for some time. I suspect this particular stone started as a very small piece of personal skulduggery and was discovered and turned legit. Although it all sounds highly unlikely, more surprising things have turned up in the past when companies have had to suffer an investigation in their accounting, for one reason or another. Sutton simply tidies the matter up.

SUTTON TO BANISTER (PERSONAL)

Dear Mr. Banister, 23.7.70

LABWELS Gerry & Johns

Thank you for drawing my attention to the question of the extra discount allowed by Gerry & Johns under certain circumstances. It was just as well that you did.

As a result of your letter I had a talk with Mrs. Beeton who gave me details of the arrangement they have with G & J, for which there are good reasons. They are quite strict, however, about where payments into this account emanate from. In this particular case, the discount should not go there. It is also better that it does not go to Rubicon as a discount received by you under the contract which should be passed on to the employer. I am afraid this only leaves one option open, namely for you to retain it. I hope you will not find that too hard to agree on!

Since this is all with the full knowledge of the employer there is no reason why it should appear in the costs records at all. If, by any chance, the Quantity Surveyors come across it and raise a query please refer them to me. It sounds to me like an appropriate sum to put towards the opening ceremony!

Yours sincerely,

All this messing about with discounts sounds rather stupid. The intention in the contract is that when a builder quotes a price, that price should include his expected profit and no more. He should not be pricing on the expectancy of getting extra profit in the shape of undisclosed discounts, although this practice is rife in some areas.

28
The Gold Rush

DRAUGHTSMAN TO SUTTON (PERSONAL)

Dear Richard, 26.7.70

LABWELS

George Turvy has had a preliminary word with me about the opening ceremony. I gather the Chairman would like a proper official function and is going to ask Sir Leslie Shovel, the Minister for Industry, to perform the usual honours. Mr. Turvy is happy to leave it to you to arrange the details and I am to give you what assistance you require.

As there will be some ladies present, mainly the wives of the official party and Dora Beeton, Mr. Turvy has asked his wife to help us out on that side of things. I understand you have already met her socially a couple of times, so perhaps it would be best if you were to make the first approach and arrange a date for all three of us to meet for a preliminary talk.

The actual date of the ceremony has still to be fixed, but to be on the safe side as regards K & B's ability to finish, I suggest it should not be earlier than the last week of September.

Looking forward to hearing from you,

Yours sincerely,

SUTTON TO MRS. TURVY

Dear Mrs. Turvy, 28.7.70

I understand from Leslie Draughtsman of Rubicon that you have very kindly consented to help us in our arrangements for the official opening of the new laboratory and welfare building. Although the actual date of the ceremony has yet to be fixed, the last week of September seems likely and we must therefore begin to make our plans now.

Without wishing to impose unduly on your time, I feel we ought to allow for perhaps three or four meetings. To begin with, I wonder whether you could manage a couple of hours at my office on 1st August at 2.00 p.m.? Leslie has already told me he can make that date.

Very best wishes,

Yours sincerely,

NOTES ON A MEETING HELD AT THIS OFFICE ON 1.8.70 TO CONSIDER THE ARRANGEMENTS TO BE MADE FOR THE OPENING CEREMONY

Present: Mrs. T. Turvy
L. Draughtsman
R. J. Sutton

1. R. J. Sutton outlined the general situation. He said the building would be ready for occupation in roughly two months time, and that a safe date for the opening ceremony would be at the end of September. Agreed that the 29th be suggested to Rubicon's management.

2. The first step would be to get this date firmly confirmed all round, and especially by the Chairman, Sir Sidney Rough, who would in turn have to agree it with Sir Leslie Shovel, the Minister for Industry.

3. The proceedings to take the form of cutting a tape and opening the door with a golden key. Mrs. Turvy said the golden key was an important element as it caught the attention of the Press. Present Yale-type lock not suitable, so extra lock to be fitted.

4. Scissors also required to cut type (also golden?).

5. Should the Minister's wife also participate, eg cut the tape and he to turn the key?

6. A plaque will be needed. Lettering to go on it to be agreed (who with?). Will a curtain with a drawstring be required (another job for someone, perhaps the Mayor but more likely Lady Shovell instead of the tape). Or is this all a bit too much?

7. Tour of building to be arranged. Several guides needed to keep parties down to say 8 or ten in size. Mrs. Turvy to conduct the Ladies (they may need the powder room). NO this is Dora Beeton's province and Mrs. T. must not fall foul of her. Best keep Mrs. Turvy to the Labs. She will have to do her homework with Dr. Science first, and is familiar enough with what happens there not to be caught out by any smart Alec.

8. Numbers to be established as soon as possible. Mrs. Beeton will do the catering and will need to know. L.D. could offer no guidance at all but will 'ask his dad'. Mrs. B. will have to sort out her kitchen capability with Bains Marie well before the date.

9. Tasks to be undertaken now. R.J.S. to make enquiries with

Mrs Turvy said the golden key was an important element. . .

jewellers re gold key and scissors, and with engravers re plate. Also to go into detail re completion with K and B and establish a firm possible date. L.D. to check on date for chairman and official party; also anticipated size of party (A) for drinks, and (B) for drinks and luncheon. Settle times and constitution of official VIP party. T.T. To see Dr. Science about tour of Labs and Mrs. Beeton about tour of canteen etc and arrangements for the luncheon party. Check with L.D. on number of ladies.
10. That was all the business and it was agreed to meet again in a week's time same time and place.

NOTES ON A MEETING HELD AT THIS OFFICE ON 8.8.70 TO CONTINUE THE PROGRAMME OF ARRANGEMENTS FOR THE OPENING CEREMONY

Present: Mrs. T. Turvy
L. Draughtsman
R.J.S.

1. Mr. Draughtsman began by saying that a delicate position had just arisen that morning which he felt he should report immediately. He said it appeared that in giving instructions to go ahead and arrange the opening ceremony, Mr. Turvy had overlooked the fact that in matters such as these, the job of arranging public ceremonies should have gone automatically to 'Prop' Steadman as a polite recognition of his seniority and his many years of service with the company. To avoid causing unnecessary offence, Mr. Turvy consequently felt those present should lie low as if nothing much had happened, but keep discreet contact with any arrangements already underway. Mr. Turvy felt the present arrangements would be ultimately needed, as it was unlikely that Prop Steadman would have any fixed ideas as to who should do what. However, Mr. Turvy would be consulting Prop about the guest list as a matter of courtesy and he felt that would probably suffice.
2. Each member then reported on the progress so far, but there was little to report. R.J.S. had placed enquiries for the plaque and discussed progress with Knott & Banister. He had also made enquiries at Schwulstig the jewellers about the cost of a gold key and scissors. Mrs. Turvy would finalise the buffet and luncheon menus with Mrs. Beeton the following day. Mrs. Turvy stressed that firm information about catering numbers was now a matter of extreme urgency.

3. Under the circumstances, it was agreed there would be no point in meeting again until Prop Steadman and George Turvy produced the guest list, but it was generally felt that what had been so far achieved would come in useful.

29

The Final Inspection

DRAUGHTSMAN TO SUTTON

Dear Richard, 8.8.70

LABWELS

You may have noticed that Bomber Harris has been uncharacteristically quiet recently. He is in fact preoccupied with something that has always been a fetish of his, viz. the final inspection. During the past week he has been wandering round the job with a preoccupied expression and a notebook, which I notice is now almost full. This is the sort of job he really gets his teeth into and I think I should warn you that what comes out at the end is likely to be very extensive.

Although I can recognise a good bit of brickwork when I see it, I am not trained either as an architect or tradesman. I thought, therefore, that a final inspection should be done in conjunction with the builder and that the architect should at least be notified that it is in progress. As nothing has passed through my hands I assume you have not been.

Yours sincerely,

MEMO FROM HIGGINS TO SUTTON RE LABWELS

9.8.70

The last time I paid a visit to the site I looked for Bomber Harris and found him engaged on a final inspection. As we have not been notified I queried this and the gist of his four-letter reply was that in his experience architects were * * * * useless on final inspections – all they saw were light fittings, ventilation grilles, convectors and * * * * radiators. He has notified K & B who put a foreman with him, but the amount of detail floored even him to the extent that after three days he gave up on the principle it would be easier to wait until the report is on paper. Personally, I suspect this is just another piece of Bomber-type psychological warfare and that we should not worry too much about it.

Let us hope so. The so-called final inspection is always a hell of a bind, especially in multi-unit buildings such as blocks of flats where everything is repeated some hundreds of times. Fortunately, this is not the case here, nor is this the final inspection in precise terms. That cannot take place until the contract maintenance period has expired (usually six months) and any reported defects have been dealt with. It is, however, usual and necessary for an inspection to be made before the owner takes possession. This is usually quite detailed, especially as to things which should be dealt with during the maintenance period. Very fine detail is reserved for the post maintenance inspection, which is the last occasion for the employer to get anything further from the contractor, both of whom are by then heartily sick of each other and with the architect.

STEELE OF KNOTT & BANISTER TO SUTTON

Dear Sir, 9.8.70

LABWELS

We confess to a degree of apprehension about the present activities of Mr. Harris, who is compiling a final inspection report. This, when it is finished, is going to be a monster and we cannot envisage that we have made the number of errors which would require a report of this size.

Mr. Harris did inform us that he was starting this procedure, should we care to have someone go over it with him. I did, in fact, agree to spend the first morning with him, but at the end of the day we were still in same room. We then put our foreman on the job, but after three days, he could stick it no longer and the job was suffering. As there are a lot of things happening at the moment, we gave it up and propose now to wait for the finished result. So far as I know we have not made any more or any less boobs on this job than on any other and we think it represents a fair standard of what can be expected of a building today.

We really have no qualms, but thought we should let you know what is going on.

Yours faithfully,

By now Sutton must be waiting with considerable apprehension for the dreaded report, rather as though it were a letter bomb, which from Harris would be appropriate. He has not long to wait.

TURVY TO SUTTON

Dear Richard, 15.8.70

LABWELS. Final Inspection

When Harris supervises a job for us he usually makes a very thorough final inspection, so that everything not in order is listed. I gather he informed the builder of his intention but that after the first day or so they pleaded other duties, and seemed to think the inspection was a time-wasting and unnecessary procedure. Harris should also have informed you but from what Leslie says, I gather he didn't.

The report is now finished and I am enclosing three copies; one for you, one to pass on to the builder and one spare. If you should need any more please let me know and they will be supplied.

I have not gone through the report in detail, because as you see it is rather lengthy, but it seems to be set out in a coherent manner having been taken room by room, plus the exterior and external works. I am confident that Harris is knowledgable about all the building trades and that his observations will be clearly understood.

Please let me have your own views.

Yours sincerely,

SUTTON TO TURVY

Dear George, 17.8.70

LABWELS. Final Inspection

Thank you for your letter and the three copies of Harris's 'final inspection' report. Although he had not informed me, I had information from three different sources that it was in progress and what it might contain.

My observations are as follows:

1. It is not really a final report, because such an inspection cannot be done until after the conclusion of the defects liability period.

2. The report is certainly comprehensive, but too much so for ease of understanding. It is presented on a room-by-room basis

which, although it is the easiest way for the compiler of the report and produces maximum bulk, is not the easiest way for the builder who has to remedy the items complained of.

3. The best way to present such a report is on a trade-by-trade basis, so that the builder can hand each trade the part which concerns them and from which he can see where co-ordination of trades is required.

4. I have now put in hand the breakdown and reassembly of the report in this form which I will then distribute.

I hope you will not feel that I am trying to belittle Harris's efforts. What he has done will be useful, at least to him, because when the time comes it will assist him in checking that all has been dealt with. I think, however, that such time will truly arrive when the proper final report has to be made.

Many things which are listed at this stage are not meant to be dealt with now, because during the six months maintenance period they may well become worse, and additional things will appear. It is only fair to the contractor, and convenient for the employer, to leave minor defects so they can all be dealt with together during one visit to the site (or at least the minimum number of visits).

Yours sincerely,

This from Sutton to Turvy sounds a bit high-handed, but by now everyone (except Harris and Turvy) sees this report as a joke in rather bad taste. To expect it to be taken seriously, as Turvy seems to, is rather embarrassing. Sutton decides to go a bit further to see if the water gets any warmer as it gets deeper. It doesn't.

NOTE MADE FOLLOWING A DISCUSSION ON THE SITE WITH R. HARRIS ON 18.8.70 RE THE SUBJECT OF HIS SO-CALLED FINAL INSPECTION REPORT

1. I asked Harris to show me some of the typical defects described in his report. We had a look at a number of things, e.g. cracks in plaster, which were mainly hairline, a few cracked wall tiles, screws missing and paint defects etc., etc.

2. I enquired if it was his intention that these should all be dealt with now, prior to occupation. Apparently it is and he is going to see that they '* * * * well are'. I suggested this was not standard procedure as the faults may reappear before the

end of the maintenance period, which means doing the job twice for the builder.

3. Harris said this was no concern of his and that he was not going to have a * * * * building handed over to his chiefs in anything but A1 condition. That was his way, always had been and always would be. He told me I should get on with my * * * * job as an architect by telling everybody what they had to produce, and he would do his by seeing that they * * * * well did.

4. Leslie appeared on the site at this point and I called for his support. He agreed with me, but as he does not really have direct control of Harris whose authority comes from further up, he was not really able to take much of a stand.

5. My conclusion is we have reached an impasse.
there is no obvious route out.

SUTTON TO DRAUGHTSMAN (PERSONAL)

Dear Leslie, 19.8.70

LABWELS

As you know I had a word with Harris yesterday about his famous final inspection report, and you also saw the result. Scratch my head as I may, I cannot see any way out of this dilemma except to do nothing and see what gives. What do you think?

Yours sincerely,

DRAUGHTSMAN TO SUTTON (PERSONAL)

Dear Richard, 20.8.70

LABWELS

I agree. Leave the ball in Bomber's court and see where he kicks it next. I take it you will, in the meantime, withhold the issue of the reorganised report you are having prepared?

Yours sincerely,

Draughtsman has put his finger on a point which seems to have escaped Sutton. If he issues his reorganised version, which he has told Turvy he intends to do, it would make the implementation of the report so much easier for K. & B. This is really his duty, and we know how much that means to Sooty. This, however, would detract from his attempt to show that the implementation at this stage is not really a practical proposition. He decides to lie low for a while.

KNOTT & BANISTER TO SUTTON

Dear Sir, 21.8.70

LABWELS. Final Inspection

Mr. Harris today asked us if we had received a copy of his report which he says should have reached you via Mr. Turvy, with a copy for onward transmission to us. He is anxious we should make an immediate start correcting the items which are listed.

We have not yet seen a copy, but from what we hear, it sounds as though there is not a cat in Hell's chance of our getting through it before the official completion date.

Mr. Harris says we must press you for instructions.

Yours faithfully,

SUTTON TO KNOTT & BANISTER

Dear Sirs, 23.8.70

LABWELS. Final Inspection

Thank you for your letter. The reason for not immediately sending you a copy of the Harris report was that I did not consider it suitable as a working tool for dealing with the defects it listed. My intention was, and still is, to reorganise it into trades to enable you to pass out only those items which are relevant to each particular trade or sub-contractor.

This reorganisation is proceeding but it is a lengthy process and I am sure it cannot be completed in time for you to have the defects all dealt with by the opening date. In my opinion, it would be better not to start this process until we are into the defects period but Mr. Harris does not agree.

I now enclose a copy of his report which was intended for you in the first place. As I am sure you know, as the contractor you will have to carry out the works as specified and make good any defects, but you are entitled to do this in the way you decide is best. You are also entitled to carry out such work at an appropriate time to suit your own programme providing you hand over the job in a proper state of completion when the time comes.

I do not propose to interfere between you and the site engineer in this matter.

Yours faithfully,

KNOTT & BANISTER TO SUTTON

Dear Sir, 25.8.70

LABWELS. Final Inspection etc.

Thank you for your letter and the enclosed copy of Mr. Harris's report. We have informed him that we have now received it, but because of its length it will take us several days, perhaps a week, to study it before we can take any action to put it into operation. By that time, we will be getting quite close to the hand-over date, and it would be most inconvenient for everyone concerned if we were still messing about all over the place when an official party was being shown around.

We have also said, that in our view, he is not within his rights under the contract to tell us how to organise our work, only what has to be done, not when.

I cannot say we were popular and we are awaiting the next shot in this campaign of attrition.

Yours faithfully,

It is quite surprising just how effective a campaign of simple non-co-operation can be. The right to give orders must be backed up by an authority that will inflict punishment if these orders are not obeyed and Harris is not quite in that position. His bluff is being called, but he hasn't quite given up yet.

DRAUGHTSMAN TO SUTTON

Dear Richard, 25.8,70

LABWELS. Final Inspection

You really have got Harris hopping mad, largely because he has put himself in a situation where bad language and shouting is not going to help him. He cannot understand why these two reliable systems, which have never failed him in the past, now seem to be doing so.

He is clearly having difficulty in deciding how he can enforce obedience to his orders, which since he does not have overall control is difficult to achieve. There is only one obvious way, but this is dependent on our co-operation; viz. to cut off the money supply. He has therefore asked me to instruct (sic) you not to issue another certificate until action is taken on his instructions.

I have pointed out that I do not have the necessary authority to do this, since under the terms of your appointment with the company, it is your responsibility to see to it that certificates are issued as and when they become due under the terms of the contract. I have told him that the lowest level of authority within the company which could issue such an instruction would be George Turvy and even then it might be necessary (strictly speaking) to seek confirmation. At any rate, I have told him that I cannot, and in any case would not, take such a step. He may go to George. I am not expecting him to approach you direct because he knows it would be futile.

Yours sincerely,

Under the contract the architect has the right to withhold a certificate if the contractor is in default of their terms thereof. Such is not the case with Knott & Banister. The sort of things for which the withholding of a certificate is allowed are non-payment of sub-contractors of monies which are included in the certificate for them, or failure to carry out instructions directly issued by the architect within the terms of the contract. He is not obliged to follow the directions of a clerk of works, or even of the employer, unless these are backed up by the architect.

Harris then goes to Turvy with his tale and Turvy decides to back him although he also knows that he cannot do so over Sutton's head. He does, of course, have a powerful weapon in the shape of denying Sutton future work, but he is unlikely to go so far as this. There may be others who would have something to say.

TURVY TO SUTTON

Dear Richard, 26.8.70

LABWELS. Final Inspection

Bomber Harris has completed a final inspection, which according to his lights, is the proper way to deal with things at this stage of any job. He likes to see everything 'shipshape and Bristol fashion' and whilst I appreciate that this state of affairs is becoming more and more difficult to achieve, it is surely an ideal to aim for, and nothing can be lost by doing so.

From what he tells me, he is not receiving any encouragement from you, or indeed from members of our own staff, in getting things moving. It seems to be a case of 'you can lead a horse to water but you can't make it drink', the horse in this case being Knott & Banister, who are taking the line that they only take orders from you and such orders are not yet forthcoming.

I appreciate the facts of life are not always the way Harris interprets them, but he is only doing his job as he sees it, and ought we not to rally round and back him up? I hope you can see the justice of this approach and get K & B moving on at least the principal items in the list of defects.

Yours sincerely,

This clearly shows that Turvy, like Harris, is living in cloud-cuckoo land. His opinion (which he seems to regard as irrefutable) that 'it is surely an ideal to be worked for, and nothing can be lost by doing so', is quite untrue. A great deal can be lost.

SUTTON TO TURVY

Dear George, 28.8.70

LABWELS. Final Inspection

Thank you for your letter. At first sight, and I admire your loyalty in backing up a well-tried, old-established employee. However, I hope you will not take it amiss if I say that this very loyalty has probably cost you a great deal of money in the past, and may well do so again.

Harris is here trying to force through a procedure which he thinks has worked well in the past and he sees no reason why it should not do so again. I am afraid there are many reasons in this case why it would not work, not least of which is the fact he does not have entire control of the job in his own hands.

If you speak to Leslie he will tell you there is now no way that K & B and their sub-contractors could tackle Harris's formidable list and tidy up before the opening ceremony. This being so, it is far better that they concentrate on finishing the job properly and deal with the defects as a properly planned exercise at the end of the liability period. Everyone will profit from this method; not just the builder, but the sub-contractors and the *client too*.

So far, I have not put these views directly to Harris, nor has he made any direct approach to me. The builders, however, have expressed their view to Harris that he is out of order in trying to instruct them to get on with these tasks now, when their priority must clearly be to get the building generally ready for occupation. The timing of putting any defects to rights is the prerogative of the builder, providing such defects are dealt with at the end of the liability period. I fear this is not always appreciated.

To sum this unhappy matter up, it is my view that Harris is out of order, and I sincerely hope you will have a quiet word with him and ask him to stop making demands which he has no power to have carried out. I do assure you that K & B have all they can cope with getting everything completed in readiness for the opening ceremony.

Yours sincerely,

DRAUGHTSMAN TO SUTTON

Dear Richard, 29.8.70

LABWELS

I dread to think what you have done to put George Turvy into such a mean temper, but the mention of your opinion on defects liability sent the glass down to Stormy.

Whatever you said, I think he is resigned to accepting it, but of course, he now has to tell the Bomber he is out of line and that should lead to a display of pyrotechnics. Knott & Banister are proceding blithely as though there never was any dispute, which I suppose, from their point of view there never was.

I do not think George Turvy has replied to your letter, and I don't think he intends to. He hinted he would leave it to me to sort out the rights and wrongs of the situation and let everyone know.

Yours sincerely,

P.S. I am not sure if you noticed, but amongst the verbose detail of Harris's report there was one item that occurred with 100% regularity. It is the condition of the cork-tile floors. As you know these were specified to be thoroughly cleaned, including washing, and to be allowed to dry before sealing with a polyurethane clear plastic finish, which was reputed to have good non-slip qualities.

"It looks as though it was the work of a mural artist carefully preserved."

As you know, during the last few weeks it has been impossible to prevent more than one trade working in a room at the same time although I know it should have been. The floors were very well cleaned and washed but were later subjected to the tread of dusty boots. When the sprayers and polishers moved in they saw a certain amount of dust and tried to deal with it using a so-called 'minute mop'. This simply spread the dust about and I'm afraid the result can be seen distinctly through the clear finish of the polyurethane. It looks as though it were the work of an abstract expressionist mural artist which was being carefully preserved.

This is rather alarming, because of its widespread nature. It occurs on virtually all the cork-tile floors and so far has escaped Harris's eagle eye, because in his haste to get on with his report, he did not check that the dust had been cleaned off for the second time. When everyone moves in, it is going to be painfully obvious and will come again into the category of work that 'cannot be accepted'. We are also going to have the same problem as to who is responsible.

I am sure you take my point. There is bound to be a certain amount of unpleasantness from people who have never watched a building being built at close quarters and who fail to see why everything should not be perfect. We shall have to clean the floors down before opening day, at which point the fault is going to become painfully obvious, and we shall need a story to tell. I suppose the truth is the only thing. Even Harris will not be able to say anything because he missed it until it was too late.

SUTTON TO TURVY

Dear George, 30.8.70

LABWELS

I think Leslie will have mentioned to you the problem we have with the cork floors. This letter is to give you my own views on the matter as it is potentially a source of bad feeling which could spread to the rest of the job.

As with the problem of the screeds the responsibility for these floors is going to be difficult to place with the degree of certainty which will make it acceptable to those who are going to have to put it right. At the moment the trouble is not obvious because of the amount of dirt which is still lying about. No matter how clean a foreman tries to keep his job, new dust etc. collects every day, and even when rooms are locked it seems there is always someone who has to have a key to do something or other. However, we open soon and as the floors will have to be cleaned for that occasion, they will be seen to have dust sealed into them below the P/U sealer.

I can do nothing about this at the moment, but it will, of course, have to be picked up during the defects period, to everyone's inconvenience, I'm afraid. It is then that the problem of split responsibility will rear it's ugly head and it is going to be an expensive business. I thought you should be forewarned. Steele of K & B has developed an ulcer and I suspect that this is the reason.

Yours sincerely,

The defects if dealt with now would have to be done in indecent haste, and would still have to be done again later. The builder has a right not to be drawn into this trap, and the bad blood which it can generate may well lead to skimping the work which then has to be dealt with again, resulting in threats of withholding final payment, threats of going to arbitration and all the other attendant horrors of litigation.

TURVY TO SUTTON

Dear Richard, 30.8.70

LABWELS. Final Inspection

I have a funny feeling that I am being manoeuvred into a minority of one (or two if we count Harris) on this question. Anyway I cannot deny that the battle has now been lost by simple inertia on the part of those being jollied along. It is a powerful weapon. Whatever the situation at the time when Harris first raised the matter, there is no doubt now that nothing can be done before the opening date, apart from a few temporary cosmetics. I have told Harris this, and he accepted it with quite good grace. To him life is a battle made up of a series of skirmishes, and he can feel admiration for anyone who can beat him at his own game. I think we can call the matter closed and close ranks to get the next obstacle out of the way, viz. the opening ceremony.

Yours sincerely,

30
A Race to the Finish

STEADMAN TO SUTTON

Dear Mr. Sutton, 26.8.70

LABWELS Building. Opening Ceremony

You may be a little surprised to hear from me instead of your more usual contacts at Rubicon. The reason is that I have been here longer than any of the other senior staff and have seen the firm grow from small beginnings to what it is today. I take considerable pride in this, but like all 'old timers' I do not like to see the past forgotten.

It has become a tradition, therefore, that whenever the company makes any significant new advance involving capital outlay, I am given the job of organising such things as the guest list, commemorative plaque and golden key etc. I hope I can rely on your help.

First, and undoubtedly most important, is the condition of the building itself, which must look immaculate. Here the word is 'look', because anything not finished can be camouflaged and I have a modest fund allowed for that purpose. Anything that will eventually form part of the contract can be of course included without extra cost.

What I would like from you now is a schedule of those things that need to be done to make everything right on the day and an estimate of how long it will take to complete and the cost. I expect you will wish to consult with Knott & Banister over this and I hope you can have it ready in two days time when we can meet to discuss it.

As to the guest list, you may have a few people you would like to receive invitations, so please let me know. We have in mind a list of about fifty people headed by the Minister for Industry, Sir Leslie Shovel. It is he who will actually perform the opening ceremony.

Yours sincerely,

SUTTON TO STEADMAN

Dear Mr. Steadman, 28.8.70

LABWELS Official Opening

Thank you for your letter. Of course I will do the best I can to help you make the event a succcss. I had heard from George Turvy that the Chairman wanted a full official opening, and so I have been doing a little preliminary research along with Leslie Draughtsman and Mrs. Turvy who kindly volunteered to assist Mrs. Beeton with the domestic arrangements.

As I see it, the most important things I can do to help are:
1. To try to ensure that the building is as spic and span as humanly possible on the day. In this I know I shall have the whole-hearted support of Knott & Banister who are the sort of firm who still set store by such things as part of their reputation.
2. To bring to your attention the names of those who have been principally involved in bringing the job to completion, and who would feel a little hurt if they were not invited.
3. To provide a nameplate suitably inscribed and a ribbon (I suggest red, white and blue) to be stretched across the door with a pair of scissors to cut it with. I would suggest a plaque of satin-finished stainless steel in an ebony frame. I will prcparc a drawing for your approval. In the meantime, I give below a suggestion for the wording.
4. To provide a golden key. The actual front door lock is a cylinder type and as you know, the keys do not make a very good ceremonial object. What I propose, therefore, is to fit an extra mortise lock. Enquiries have been made about solid gold keys, but this would be difficult and extremely expensive so I propose a brass key plated in gold.
5. I expect you will want to give the Minister a commemorative present, so I suggest having the scissors also made in brass and gold-plated, the two items being presented in a leather, velvet-lined case.

As we are going to need at least three weeks for delivery of the plaque, key and scissors, an immediate decision is needed. My suggestion for the wording is shown below.

Yours sincerely,

Sutton seems to be reeling off the details like a hardened campaigner. Arranging an official opening is usually a nerve-testing affair. There are always times when the ribbon seems to be tougher than the edge of the scissors, or the drawstring on the plaque will not pull. This once happened to me when the Queen was officiating, but she clearly showed the calm of long years of experience and reaching up with both hands she separated the curtains without a sign that anything untoward had happened.

The worst things of all are items of sculpture. When even most elaborate precautions are taken, even with the aid of modern electronic technology, about half the shrouds fail to fall and someone has to make an undignified scramble up the statuary to cast the rest off.

STEADMAN TO SUTTON

Dear Mr. Sutton, 29.8.70

LABWELS Opening

Thank you for your very helpful letter. It sounds to me as though you have done this before. I appreciate the need for haste and having just had a quick word with J.J. I can therefore say yes to all your points and request you to proceed with maximum speed.

The only thing I still need from you is your list of people you would like invited. I am sorry to place a limit, but as things stand at the moment, I cannot cope with more than six. I hasten to add that these guests are in addition to yourself and Higgins, who is a nice chap and ought to be there.

Yours sincerely,

SUTTON TO STEADMAN

Dear Mr. Steadman, 31.8.70

LABWELS Opening Ceremony

Thank you for your letter. This gives me all I want to know and I have put everything to 'go' with no escape clauses for delay. I hope it all works out right on the day, but I expect there are bound to be a few last-minute panics.

As regards the list to be invited may I nominate the following:

Architects:	R. J. Sutton	
	H. Higgins	
Builders:	W. Banister	Knott & Banister
	A. Steele	

Sub-contractors:	P. Thinners	Brush & Rollerman
	S. Stover	Bains Marie Ltd.
	A. C. Norriman	Shefleford Ceramics
	E. P. Resin	Toughgrain Floors
Quantity surveyors:	J. le Mesurier	Cutt & Shuffle
Leverpullers Ltd.:	Ian McDonald	Architect

I realise this is eight and not six, but I thought you might have some Leverpullers people on your list and Mr. McDonald might be one of them. It was he, after all, who introduced me to Rubicon. I think I ought also to include James le Mesurier who, from your point of view, might be thought of as one of my office. I am sorry that I have had to leave out quite a lot of sub-contractors, but I have included those with whom we all had more direct contact because of the nature of their work.

Yours sincerely,

The compilation of this kind of list is always a pain in the neck. One cannot include everyone and even if one did, those who counted themselves well qualified for inclusion would not like it. As Gilbert so aptly said, 'When everyone is somebody, then no-one's anybody'. Inevitably, one has to be ruthless and risk receiving letters which begin, 'I was interested to read in the press yesterday, of the opening of your new building and of the ceremony attended by so many people of my acquaintance. It would have been so nice to have a chance to chat with them, etc., etc.'

TURVY TO SUTTON

Dear Richard, 14.9.70

LABWELS Opening Ceremony

I made a tour of the works today and came to the only possible conclusion I could, which was that you have made a mistake about the date of the official opening. I fear you think it is in four weeks time and not a mere ten days. I fail to see how order can be made out of the existing chaos in that time.

I asked Knott & Banister's foreman to show me his programme and he produced the one for the whole job. I said, 'Not that! I want the programme for the finishing operation!' and he said he had, 'never seen one' which means there isn't one. He then advised me not to worry, which is advice I find impossible to take.

Will you please come and see me here at 11.00 a.m. on Friday and prove to me that it can be done. I am also inviting Leslie Draughtsman on whom some of the builder's sang froid seems to have rubbed off.

Yours sincerely,

Turvy is wong. What appears to be utter chaos is really quite normal a week or so before the completion date. The general appearance of the new building is like an anthill and those of you, dear readers, who have ever watched ants' activity for any length of time will have not only noticed the frenzied rate at which operations are taking place, but the apparently totally unrelated activities of these industrious creatures.

Come with me and look into a room which yesterday appeared to have been completed. A number of the suspended ceiling tiles have been removed and there are wires hanging from the hole. A radiator which was connected has been removed and is standing to one side, whilst a painter is busy on the wall behind it. A door has been removed and is having bits shaved off the edges and the mortise latch reset. The door furniture has been slackened off for the painter. Cover plates on switches and junction boxes have been removed for the same reason and to enable last stage connections to be made. There is no worked-out detailed programme, but like nature and the ants there is a divine providence which somehow co-ordinates their activities. Sutton tries to explain.

SUTTON TO TURVY

Dear George, 15.9.70

LABWELS Opening

I am sorry if your visit to the works yesterday caused you to despair of ever seeing the job completed. Believe me, I know the feeling. There are days when progress seems to actually be in the reverse direction, and to some extent this may be said to be true. As I'm afraid I cannot make it to your office on Friday at 11.00 I do hope this letter will serve to put your mind at rest.

There are elements in the building fabric which have what is known in the trade as 'First and Second Fixing' and there is often a long period between them. Electrical installations are a case in point, where the skeleton (e.g. conduit etc.) has to be fixed early, before all the finishing trades. Later on, the wiring follows and last of all, the switches and light fittings etc. These last may have to be fixed, to ensure they fit, and then removed

The general appearance is like an anthill.

for the painter. (This is known as offering up.) There are many other items in the same category.

Like you, I like to see a programme for everything, on which I can neatly cross out those items which are finished and hence discern at a glance which items are slipping behind. I have to accept, however, that nobody can draw up a programme for what is going on at the moment on the site. It all works by means of some mysterious empathy between the tradesmen, with a little catalytic assistance from the general foreman. One hears such things as, 'Hey mate do you have to drill holes in here?' 'Yes.' 'Do it today then, 'cos I have to paint it tomorrow' and so on.

Perhaps I am sticking my neck out in saying that 'it will be allright on the night' but I really do expect it to be so.

Yours sincerely,

All this is very true. Strangely, if one had the same situation on a job that did not have any specific opening date, it would not be possible to whip up the same sense of urgency and the work would not be finished on time.

Sooty is not really 'sticking his neck out' this time because it already was out, the date having been fixed some time ago. I have seen many opening days come and go and in every case a week before, it looked impossible. A certain amount of ingenuity may have had to be used to cover up obviously unfinished bits and pieces, but one way or another the great occasion has passed off without any major disaster.

NOTE OF A TELEPHONE MESSAGE TAKEN BY BETZY PARKER AT 10.30 A.M. ON 16.9.70

Mr. Turvy telephoned while you were out this morning and left a message which reads, '*IT HAD BETTER BE. GEORGE*'. He said you would know what he meant. I think I do too! Betzy.

SUTTON TO DRAUGHTSMAN

Dear Leslie, 23.9.70

LABWELS Opening

The great day is nearly upon us and one of my big worries is over. I have heard from Schwulstig the jewellers that the gold-plated key and scissors are ready for collection. As you will be the charge de affairs on the day, it would be best if you were to collect them, to avoid slip-ups due to multi-handling. I enclose the order slip, in case you should need it. They will be in a tooled leather case with a suitable inscription.

I think it would be a good idea if you were to personally check the key in the lock to make sure that it will in fact open it. It would be embarrassing if Sir Leslie Shovel were to find himself locked out. You might also check that the scissors will cut the ribbon. It sounds farcical I know, but I actually heard of a case in which all the scissors could achieve was to fold the ribbon over between the blades and vaguely chew it. Fortunately, there was a boy scout in the audience who produced his knife!

One last point. As you know, there is also a yale-type cylinder night latch on the door, which will have to be held back by the snib provided on the inside. I would suggest that you have a trustworthy man lurking about inside during the open-air speeches who can see to it that it is open. He might also be useful in coping with anything else that might go wrong, of which we can have no possible inkling at the moment.

I would have liked to have another chat with you before the event, but I gather you have a trip to make which can't be put off, and which gets you back only twenty-four hours before the ceremony. For goodness sake, don't miss the 'plane!

I hope all this doesn't sound as though I am trying to take over. During the progress of LABWELS I have been at the wheel, as it were, but this day is definitely Rubicon's and I am only one member of a team which has worked hard to make dear old LABWELS a success.

Yours sincerely,

31

An Open Declaration

The events which occur during ceremonial occasions are usually lost to posterity as there is no organisation, such as Hansard, to record them.

This time we are fortunate, because in the general euphoria of seeing his job reach an apparently successful finish, Sutton decided, with the help of Betzy, to make a record. It reads like this:

9.00. Strong inclination to rush straight off to Labwels, but like Drake on Plymouth Hoe, resisted and dealt with usual chores. Nothing due to start until 11.30 anyway.

10.00. Frantic telephone call from a demoralised Leslie Draughtsman. He has only this moment seen my letter and now has to go to meet the chairman. Minister and Mayor due at 11.00. No time to collect packet. Said not to worry, Higgins has a scooter and can collect. Another case of 'the best laid schemes'. Rang Schwulstig – Yes, they have it. Sent Higgie off.

10.45. Time to go. What has happened to Higgie? Dear God! I recall Winterfield A.S.C. have a match with Dribbleford starting at 11.15. He will be in the inevitable snarl-up.

11.00. Arrived Rubicon in time for coffee and introductions. Leslie looking a bit pallid. He looked even worse after hearing from me. Weather kind and all assembled in time.

11.30. Chairman's speech. Sir Sydney is not given to verbosity so that didn't take long. Reference to the growth of the firm over the last twenty years and its contribution to employment and rates in the area. Also the likelihood of a larger contribution in the future.

Welcome to the minister, the Rt. Hon. Sir Leslie Shovel, and the Mayor of Winterfield amongst others.

11.40. The Minister embarked on his speech. How long could he go on? Glanced across at Leslie whose eyes were turned heavenwards in mute supplication. I prayed with him.

The minister droned on 'living standards – full employment – quality of life – better than just money – some want both' (polite laughter). Then: 'Now I had better get on with what I came here to do'. I saw Leslie whispering into the ear of J.J. who was slowly turning puce giving the impression that he was about to explode. The minister turned towards him looking puzzled. J.J. swallowed hard and opened his mouth like a goldfish, but no words emerged.

At that instant I heard the putt-putt of a scooter's engine rapidly approaching. Was rescue at hand? It was; Higgins swept up like a knight on a charger holding a parcel above his head. Leslie saw him too and nudged J.J. on the elbow. It was then simply a matter of getting the goods into the right hands and J.J. was able to chat the minister up for a minute whilst this was being organised.

11.55. The minister made short work of the tape, following up with the key, and flung open the door with such vigour that Leslie's man in reserve, who was just inside, copped a smart rap on the shins and was seen hopping away as the official party swept in. The guides took charge of their parties and the conducted tours passed off without incident. The champagne flowed freely and since the civic party, as usual, stuck to beer or scotch, there was more than enough for all. The luncheon party moved to the dining room and the drinks only guests started to drift off.

1.00. Luncheon was served and Dora Beeton had seen to it that her kitchen was the equal of any Soho gourmet's haunt. She herself was seated next to the Minister and he was clearly intrigued. Should Rubicon ever want any favours from the Board of Trade, or whatever name they now answer to, they could not choose a better ambassador than Mrs. B.

After the toasts, coffee, brandy and cigars J.J. made a short speech to round off, when he thanked those (including your truly) for their part in the operation. After that the Minister made his exit, no doubt on to some other engagement. When ministers are persuaded out of their lairs they usually like to kill several birds with one stone. Others began to drift away, but there was a hard core of seasoned ceremony attenders, who would no doubt be there for as long as there was anything left to drink.

At this stage I came up with Leslie who by now was mellow. The key crisis had left him in a state of nervous exhaustion which he had sought to remedy with the help of the grape. He had succeeded. Everything now was for the best in the best of all possible worlds. 'Venga con migo' he said airing his Spanish which he was currently learning at nightschool (something to do with a project in Catalonia). I followed him into the senior staff room to which some of the supplies had thoughtfully been diverted. There I found Steele, Harris, le Mesurier, Bracket and a few others all in high good humour, and now, after the battle was over, the best of friends (if only for a day).

"To all those who will use it."

32
A Letter to Frame

BOFFIN TO SUTTON

Dear Mr. Sutton,
LABWELS Building

As the Managing Director of this company, you may have thought I would have shewn a more direct interest in what you have designed and built to fulfil certain of our needs. That I have not done so does not imply any lack of interest on my part, merely my very necessary preoccupation with other matters.

Since we originally appointed you to this task, you have obviously been the subject of discussion in senior staff circles and the tone has always been approving. As you may have been aware, our views about architects had become pretty jaundiced and I can say that you have restored our faith in your profession.

Now that our beautiful new building has been successfully completed and opened, I felt it was time someone expressed our thanks for way the job has been handled. Within that I include the expert analysis of our needs, the patience with which you have dealt with our quirks, and the conversion of an idea into a building which not only meets our requirements very well but is pleasing to the eye.

You are already engaged upon another project which I believe is going well and I hope we shall have still more opportunities to call upon your services in future. This seems most likely as we are shortly embarking on a major expansion project, designed to double our present output and diversify our products.

Yours sincerely,

This is a very handsome letter indeed from someone who is probably not given to praise on this scale very often. Sutton should be, and no doubt was, very pleased to have it. He will especially like the prospect of future work.

It would be well for him to remember that this is a 'honeymoon phase'. He will probably never again work as hard at a job for Rubicon as he has this time, with his desperate desire to impress. We have also seen the first signs of an enlargement of the practice and if it grows there will inevitably come a time when either an assistant or a junior partner will be going along to discuss a new project with Rubicon. Equally inevitably, Rubicon will not like it. They will want to deal with the man they first appointed.

This seems a good place at which to close this narrative. J.J.'s letter was, in any case, the last one in this file, but as we close it we realise there are many strands which must lead into another file somewhere. There is still a lot of work to be done in correcting defects and making changes, the need for which will only show up when the building has been occupied for some time. Details of extra costs and savings all have to be settled. The final settlement could well take a year, or even more, and use up as much paper as what has gone before. Perhaps at some future date, we might get a chance to have a look at the records of what might be just as interesting a phase as the one that has just closed.

Glossary of Building Terms

The following is a list of terms and names in common use in the architectural and building world, which have appeared in these pages. They are placed in alphabetical order, but where several items refer to the same general field they are grouped together.

BAINS-MARIE Piece of kitchen equipment containing deep vessels surrounded by hot water (literally 'Mary's bath').

BILL OF QUANTITIES (BOQ) A list of all the materials and labour needed to complete the building.

BRIEF The client's instruction, setting out his detailed requirements for the proposed building.

CERTIFICATE The total value of the work completed at any particular date.

CLERK OF WORKS The employer's representative on site to ensure that the works are properly carried out.

COMPO Cement and sand mixed 1 to 3 (by volume).

CONDITIONS OF ENGAGEMENT The rules laid down by the RIBA (see below) under which the architect must operate.

CONDITIONS OF CONTRACT The form of contract accepted by the professions and trades within the construction industry. Virtually every project of any size is controlled by them.

CONTINGENCY SUM A sum of money included in the contract to cover possible extra costs (often 5% of the contract sum).

CONTINUITY BARS Connecting reinforcing bars used across beams where floors are continuous.

CURTAIN WALLING A form of building enclosure where the walls, usually metal and glass panels, play no part in supporting floors and roof. In effect a continuous window with glazed or solid panels where appropriate.

DOE Department of the Environment. Controls many matters concerning building, including the Building Regulations.

ELECTRICS The electrical installation.

EXTRAS Items not included in the original contract price.

FINAL ACCOUNT The sum finally paid for the job after the adjustment of the price for all alterations.

FLOATING The final trowelling off to a smooth surface.

I/C In charge of.

J C T JOINT CONTRACTS TRIBUNAL A body comprised of architects, qss' and other members of the building industry whose function is to agree and maintain a 'standard form of contract'.

KSP Term used in painting timber: KNOT, STOP, PRIME. Seal knots with shellac, stop holes with filler, apply priming coat.

LETTER OF INTENT An instruction to proceed with certain work for which an official order will follow in due course.

LIPPING A condition in which part of the surface stands a little above or below another.

MAIN CONTRACTOR The builder in charge of the whole operation, who employs:

> SUB-CONTRACTORS Employed to deal with special subtrades such as plumbing, heating and electrics. Some subcontractors are appointed by the architect ('nominated'); and some by the builder. But both are *employed* by the Builder.

SUPPLIERS Supply specific items not involving work on site, eg door furniture and windows.

MAINTENANCE PERIOD The period following the occupation of the building, after which the contractor must correct any defects which have appeared after (or before) handing over. The period is usually six months but can be more.

MD Managing Director.

MSAAT Member of the Society of Architectural and Associated Technicians.

NIGHT LATCH A spring loaded cylinder ('yale') lock, which can be closed without a key.

NOMINATED SUB-CONTRACTORS Those sub-contractors nominated by the architect (see above).

P C SUM Prime cost sum. A sum included in the Bill of Quantities by the architect or qs to allow for the cost of certain items which cannot be correctly estimated at that time.

PROVISIONAL SUM Similar to P C Sum.

P/U Polyurethane; used in paint.

QUANTITY SURVEYOR One who prepares the BoQ (see above), measures variations, and agrees the final price (amongst other things).

RENDER Like plaster, but of sand and cement.

REGS A common abbrevation for Building Regulations.

RIBA The Royal Institute of British Architects.

RUNNING SAND Saturated sand which moves unless contained.

RETENTION SUM A percentage of the cost kept back from each payment (by certificate), and released at the end of the project.

SCALE OF FEES A minimum scale issued by the RIBA with which all its members are obliged to comply, to avoid 'under-cutting'.

SCREED A layer, usually sand and cement, applied to floor slabs to provide a smooth base for floor finishes.

SETTLEMENT (1) Movement of foundations due to the load above. Usually very slight. (2) The final agreement after all variations have been measured.

TENDER An offer from a builder or specialist to carry out specified work for an agreed sum: a quotation.

THIN BED A way of fixing tiles using a thin layer of mastic instead of a thick layer of cement.

TEST BORES Borings in the ground used to find out the nature of the sub-soil.

UNPROTECTED AREA A term used in the Building Regulations to define the area of an external wall which is not fire resisting (eg windows).

VARIATIONS Alterations to the amounts included in the original BOQ (see above), comprising:

EXTRAS An increase.

OMISSIONS A reduction.

WINDY HAMMER A pneumatic drill.